Journey
in
Authority

A Theological Novel

Richard P. Belcher

ISBN 1-883265-11-8

Richbarry Press

P.O. Box 302   Columbia, S.C. 29202
803-798-6800   FAX 803-798-3190

Printed in the United States of America

CONTENTS

1

Finally Peace....?

I had never really desired to start a church, but it seemed I had no other choice in 1972 when providential events clearly dictated the necessity.[1] After several months of the most trying and frightening circumstances one could ever imagine, I found myself pastor of a new church---a split from the First Baptist Church of Collegetown.

I must admit there was something refreshing about a new work. There was a spiritual atmosphere, a new spirit, a unifying love, a new freedom to worship and preach, and a glorious vision of the future---something I had never known at First Baptist Church. Yes, finally my heart was at peace, and I could continue my educational quest while I pastored this body of sixty or so dedicated believers. It seemed I would never have to worry about division in the body again.

Even the deacons and I, as we led the church were in a unique relationship, which surely had been cemented by what we had been through together at the previous church.

Ah, but the devil never rests! He may give peace and tranquility for some months (a time which can even lull a church into a blind complacency), but he surely knows when and where to strike even the unified group of believers, and many times in a place or manner we could never begin to imagine.

Such was the case at our new church---Unity Baptist Church.

It all began rather innocently when two of my deacons, Bob Motley and Sam Booker, approached me about one of their relatives preaching in our church, a Billy Motley, a nephew, to be specific. It wasn't that I had to be gone, but Bob and Sam explained their nephew was young in the ministry, would be visiting for a weekend, and that we might encourage him by hearing him speak. It all sounded so innocent!

I really would rather not have opened my pulpit to one I had never heard preach, but Bob and Sam assured me he was sound in the faith and he would edify and strengthen the church. I took their word, and rationalized that a man could not do serious damage to us in just one service. There seemed no good reason to deny the request, and since I did not want to hurt or offend Bob and Sam and their families, I agreed. And I reasoned further, it would give me a break from the pulpit for one service.

When the day arrived, I took note that the nephew was in our Sunday morning service. He seemed rather passive during my message, and to be honest, I tried to read him. A few words with him after my sermon didn't help me any further. He seemed quiet and withdrawn, shy and even humble, which caused me to conclude that Sunday evening would be quiet and uneventful as well.

But the evening service was far from placid and dull. For one thing he spoke for an hour and a half---my usual time in the pulpit was thirty-five to forty minutes, or maybe an hour on something really special. But the time element was not the worst part. I wish it had been! It was his subject and the attitude with which he spoke.

He addressed us on the subject of church government and told us flat-out that we were absolutely and undeniably disobedient to God in the matter of our church government, and that God could not bless us until we adopted scriptural principles of elder rule in our church (we had deacon/pastor leadership with congregational rule). If he said it once, he said it two dozen times, "God will never bless this mess you call a church as long as you rebel against Him and refuse to install elder rule!"

I must admit I was tempted to rise to my feet and stop Rev. Billy Motley several times, and I certainly had reason to do so. He was arrogant and abusive in his attitude. He was repeating himself. He was riding a hobby horse. He was blatantly overtime, at least according to our usual time of service. And also, I was convinced he was unscriptural in what he was saying.

The more I sat still the more I boiled inside.

"What a jerk, this Billy Motley!" I thought. "Who does he think he is to come in here and act like that? What audacity to seek to correct us in one evening! He should have come in and sought to exalt Christ. If he had a problem with what we were doing, why couldn't he have approached us in a humble manner?"

It was all I could do to close the service without saying something, rebuking at least his attitude. I could sense a grieving of the Holy Spirit, and found it difficult to pray when I closed the service. People scattered quickly, hardly speaking to me, to him or to one another---except for his family. They stayed glorying in Billy's message, congratulating him for his doctrine and even his boldness (I called it arrogance) to speak the truth, as they called it. I found out later that he had spent the entire weekend indoctrinating them in his view.

When Terry (my wife) and I got in the car, we drove silently through the dark night for several miles before we broke the silence. Then we both spoke at the same time and asked the same question.

"Well, what did you think of that?"

And then as I analyzed my heart, I came to see that was the wrong question. The real question should be, "What did God think of that?"

---

[1]See Richard P. Belcher, *A Journey in Purity* (Columbia, SC: Richbarry Press, 1990).

What Does God Think....?

As I originally spoke that question, I almost spoke in jest. But as I pondered it through the evening further, I had to conclude that was the right question---what did God think of that?

I certainly don't claim to be able to fathom the mind of God, but as I thought through it, I decided there were several possibilities:

(1) the speaker was <u>right</u> in his attitude and <u>right</u> in his message;

(2) or the speaker was <u>wrong</u> in his attitude and <u>wrong</u> in his message;

(3) or the speaker was <u>right</u> in his attitude and <u>wrong</u> in his message;

(4) or the speaker was <u>wrong</u> in his attitude and <u>right</u> in his message.

Several other questions shot through my mind.

Could it be that God would allow the truth to be delivered through a messenger with a wrong and rotten attitude?

Could it be that I might reject the truth because of a focus on the attitude of the messenger instead of a focus on the content of the message?

I had already concluded that the attitude of the messenger was wrong, and now these thoughts convinced me that the attitude of the messenger must not be the focus. I must focus on the truth or falsity of the message and not on the attitude of the messenger. As I framed the basic question, it was, "What does the Bible teach about church government?"

Even if Billy Motley had not handled the content in the best way, I still had to face the basic question---what does the Bible teach about church government? Does it teach elder rule, or does it teach congregational rule?

Clearly my mind had been challenged with another quest, and I concluded I would pursue it as I had the previous two subjects.[1] I would ask others to share with me their convictions of the teaching of Scripture, to get an idea of each view point, and then I would go to the Scripture to determine its statement on the subject.

As I flipped through my Bible at home later in the evening, I knew the Scriptures spoke of deacons, pastors, elders, and bishops. I read some of the passages which mentioned these officers (I had read them before, but had never put it all together).

Then some questions hit me? Where does the New Testament speak of congregational rule? Where does the Bible speak of deacons serving as spiritual leaders of the church? Does the Bible teach one pastor was to lead the church?

Being a member of a denomination known as the Evangelistic Baptists, I had accepted their convictions about church government almost without question. The usual pattern was for the church to be led by a single pastor and a group of deacons (other ordained ministers sometimes served under this pastor in various capacities). But even then the pastor and deacons did not have final authority on matters, for all decisions had to come before the church for a final approval by a vote.

To be honest, I (and others I had come to discover) had real misgivings about the monthly business meeting, and with the idea that every member (including children not even in their teens) was allowed to vote on almost every matter considered by the church. I had heard many horror stories about how God's people had acted in such meetings, and had seen it also in my ministry.

But again, the question had to be, "What does the Bible teach?" Doctrine must never be decided by pragmatic concerns, but only on a Scriptural basis. What is best (best from the human stand point) for the church, or what works, or what presents the least amount of problems, or what does my church or denomination believe, or what do we assume the Bible teaches, can never be the reasons for holding to a doctrinal conviction.

It must be only and always, what does the Bible teach? And I had to admit, sometimes that is not an easy question to answer!

---

[1] See Richard P. Belcher, *A Journey in Grace* and *A Journey in Purity* (Columbia, SC: Richbarry Press, 1990).

We Must Have an Elder-led Church or Else....!

Several days had passed since the previous unnerving events, but I was still fighting my agitation when Bob Motley, the uncle of my agitator, called asking me to have breakfast with him. He sounded serious, and I began to wonder if the hoped-for tranquility of Unity Baptist Church was soon to be broken and we would end up fighting over this newly discovered subject. I was convinced that our enemy never rested, and if he could not stir one issue, he would raise another.

Thus the next morning I found myself at one of the local diners having breakfast with a very serious man. He seemed quite nervous and eager to get to the point of his concern, but he did wait until we had ordered breakfast. Finally, he blurted it out.

"Pastor, we've got to become an elder-led church!"

I asked him why, and he replied, "If we do not, we are out of God's will in starting this church, and God can never bless us!"

I thought to myself that I had asked a simple question and now I had a simple answer---God cannot bless a church which is not led by elders! Or to put it another way, God cannot bless a congregationally ruled church!

I didn't want to be harsh in pinning him in debate, but I had to ask some questions in a very tender way.

"Are you sure of what the Bible teaches on this subject. Could you, right now, turn in the Bible and present and fully explain to me the Biblical evidence of the necessity of an elder-led church? Could you tell me what an elder-led church is and how it functions? Could you tell me how to implement elder rule in our church when all our people have ever known is congregational rule? Do you think an elder-led church comes by one deacon and a pastor saying this is the way it is going to be? Don't you think we need to study this matter as deacons and understand what we are doing (if we do go to elder rule) rather than jumping off a bridge into the murky waters of a new system of church government without knowing what it is or how it works?"

I could have said more, but paused to test his reaction. I found he did not surrender his case easily. He replied to me with some frustration.

"Pastor, this is not a matter to be stalled! This the future of our church!"

Then he pulled his last card from his hand as he threatened, "I can't stay if we don't move to elder rule."

In my heart I smiled! I wanted to put him on the spot. I wanted to ask him where he would go to church. I didn't know of a single Baptist church in our area that had elder-rule, and I knew he was a staunch Baptist. But I rejected this temptation concerned he might be offended. Instead I asked him to be patient.

"Bob, here is my suggestion. Remember how we studied church discipline as a deacon body? And do you remember how we sought out the teaching of the Word of God? Why can't we do that again on the subject of church government? Then at the end of the study, if the Bible teaches elder-rule, we will have a conviction and a foundation based on the Bible to take to the whole church for their study and consideration. This way we can handle the matter in a wise and diligent manner and not risk tearing up the church due to ignorance or impatience."

As he answered, I still sensed an impatience, but nonetheless he agreed to my suggestion. I promised we would raise the matter at our next deacons' meeting.

As I settled down to finish my breakfast in peace (I had been eating but had no consciousness of the process nor of the taste of the food), my old buddy Todd walked in. Todd was pastor of the Lime Creek Baptist Church, the first church I had pastored, and an old room mate in my early days of college. He sat down by us and was his usual bubbly self. Then he laid on us a shocker!

"Guess what?" he asked, with his sly, know-it-all grin. "We're going to elder rule in our church!"

I chuckled out loud, which may not have been understood by Todd. My thought was that Brother Bob would have an elder-led church to attend now, if ours didn't move to that conviction.

More pressing to my mind was what had led Todd to that conviction and determination.

Free to Search the Word....!

After I had gotten over the initial shock, I asked the expected questions.

"Todd, whatever brought you to the conviction that you need to move your church from congregational rule to an elder rule government?"

His answer was unexpected, but understandable when he stated, "Oh man, we had the greatest speaker a few weeks ago who convinced me of the need."

I wondered in my mind if the speaker could possibly be the same man who had accosted our church with such a lousy attitude and bold conviction.

Sure enough, he had been convinced by Bob Motley's nephew, Billy Motley, by the preaching of one sermon. And he had no problem with his attitude, rather he raved over Billy's boldness, which he took as a sign of the man and message being from God. Todd was convinced, and he was going to take the matter to his deacons insisting the move to elder rule be made. They would then take it to the church as soon as possible.

I tried to reason with him of the foolishness of such a quick move. I wondered if all the deacons would agree. I knew it would be confusing to the church when they had known only congregational rule through all their history. Nothing I said seemed to dampen his plan. I realized that this was so much like Todd---impulsive to the hilt. I feared for the church and fallout to come.

As a friend to Todd and to his people, who had been my people, I did something I knew would either help him or harm our relationship---but I felt it was worth the risk. I pulled out my small New Testament and asked him to show me a case for elder rule in the New Testament. It wasn't that I was against such a system of government, but it seemed clear that he was romping off into the stratosphere of doctrinal belief without chart or compass in hand.

He was upset, even embarrassed. Sheepishly, he acknowledged he wasn't ready to do so, but he had studied the matter and would defend his position at the proper time.

I noted his word "defend." I tried again to reason with him to present the matter in an objective way so the church could be educated, which would allow them to ask questions. I argued that he could not force the issue upon them for that would put them on the defensive, and they would never be open to his conviction.

However, nothing I said seemed to make any difference. He was determined to do it his way. As he left the restaurant I could tell our fellowship was strained, but I urged him to keep in touch and let me know how things were going. I hoped he would do so that I might temper and guide him.

With a sad heart I turned back to Bob Motley. He hung his head and seemed reluctant to talk. Finally he blurted out his burden.

"Pastor, I want to apologize for the attitude I had when I called, and when we first started talking this morning. In seeing Todd's plan and immaturity and impatience, I understand the wisdom of your plan. Please know I am behind you one hundred per cent. I admit I need to know what the Bible teaches about this issue. Maybe I have jumped to conclusions. I will look eagerly to studying the matter in our deacons' meetings. Will you forgive me?"

As I drove home, I marveled at God's providential ways. He had used Todd with his improper plan and attitude to solve a problem in my church. Now I rejoiced because we were free to move forward to study the Word of God and find God's will in the matter!

I continued to be burdened for Todd and the Lime Creek Baptist Church.

Pasta, You Da Man....!

It is truly amazing how one small event can stir an abundance of speculation and rumors in a church body. Nothing official had been done concerning changing our church government, nor had we even indicated any such possibility, but rumors were flying about like airplanes at a major airport.

The first inkling of such rumors was when I ran into Dink, the converted gang leader, one of the few blessings from our past experience at First Baptist Church. He was his usual self, as he dropped by my office, and began to speak admiringly of the possibility of elder rule.

"Pasta," he said, "I sure like dat guy who zinged us last Sunny night!"

I asked him what it was he liked, and found out, for one thing, he liked his style.

"Wow," Dink said admiringly, "he put it to us! He tell us right from da word! He not 'fraid of us nor nobody! He speak da trut! I like dat!"

When I asked him what truth he spoke, he was forceful again in his reply.

"Preacha, you da man! You need to be in full control! You know da book! You need to tell us what to do and back it up wit your autority---jus' like he said in elder rule. Its just like my old gang used to be! I was da boss! Somebody got to be da boss! What kinda gang is it widout a boss? Jus' like da mafia---somebody gotta crack heads---spiritually speakin, dat is. Somebody gotta intimidate! Somebody gotta apply da brass knucks, again speakin spiritually. Dat's what da man say Sunday night. I like it! We need dat elder stuff! You get dat and da Dink will help you enforce it!"

I had to smile---it was pure Dink in language and theology. But clearly he could have used a lot more knowledge of Scripture for its foundation and content.

He continued.

"Dat's what was wrong at Big Baptist Church [his term for First Baptist Church from which our church came]. Dey had da inmates over der runnin da penitentiary. Any body knows dat won't work. I know! I was in da pen a few years. Its da same in da church! Da monkeys can't run da zoo---dey need trainers and overseers. Can ya imagine, Preacha, a zoo run by da monkeys and baboons? No wonder da churches are in such a mess---we got da babies runnin da nursery!"

Again, I smiled at his descriptive manner of analyzing and explaining the situation. And, too, I was convinced I could never reason with such strange logic. But he did raise a point---to whom falls the responsibility of leading the church? Does the responsibility fall to the people, or the leaders, or a combination of both? Could part of the problem at First Baptist Church have been that we did have the monkeys running the zoo in a sense? Was there a lack of spiritual leadership among the chosen leaders and too much authority of each member? Was there a danger in the babies running the nursery?

I left my conversation with Dink praising God for the grace that had saved him, and an appreciation for his attempt to think on the problem. But again the question must be, what saith the Scriptures, and with this Dink did agree, though he had trouble understanding and interpreting the Word of God.

I prayed God would guide us all in our thinking and searching of the Word of God, including Dink.

All Elders are Dictators....!?

I didn't expect to talk to any one else on the subject of elder rule, as I assumed no one but a few had any desire to make the matter an issue, though there was discussion about it. Therefore, I was a little surprised at the phone call I received just after Dink left.

It was one of my fine loyal ladies, Mrs. Palmer, who was very sweet and humble in her life and deportment. With hesitancy she raised a very strong concern---a concern from the other side of the question.

"Pastor, I have a deep burden to share with you today. I hope you won't think I am too forward, but I had to call!"

Not having any idea of her problem, I urged her to share her concern with me, and I assured her I would listen.

"Well, I'm really disturbed over the sermon last Sunday night," she began, to which I responded with a hearty, "Amen!"

Being assured that she was not out in left field in her assessment of the matter, she continued.

"I have heard some in our church want to move to elder rule, and that frightens me. I have been a member of a Baptist Church for years, and Baptists have always had congregational rule. I am afraid elder rule will take away our rights and freedoms as Christians, as Baptists, as church members and as Americans."

To be honest, I didn't know how or why she lumped all these categories together---what does being an American have to do with the Biblical government of a local church? But I said nothing at this point, and she continued.

"I am afraid of elders wanting to rule our lives in areas in which they have no business. I have the Holy Spirit living in me and He will guide me. I don't need elders to tell me how to live. I believe in the priesthood of every believer, which means each one of us should have a part in the life and ministry and decisions of the church, and not just an elevated few! So please, Pastor, don't let them go to elder rule---it will ruin our new little church, and I don't think I could go through another church split or problems like we had at First Baptist Church!"

She was close to tears, so I quickly assured her that we had no plans to go to elder rule at this point, but that we would study it. I urged her to study the matter in her Bible and share with me what she found---elder rule or congregational rule? I asked her to seek to prove from Scripture the fact of congregational rule.

She did seem much calmer when we parted, but I admitted she had a point---any form of church government had to balance delicately the place of leadership and the lives of the people of God.

Elder rule could be a dictatorship and congregational rule could be anarchy!

Caught in the Middle....!

My arrival home that evening was rather normal, as to the hour and greeting from my wife, Terry.

"Well, how did your day go?" she innocently queried.

I didn't know whether to answer honestly or with a usual, "Just fine." I decided to stir her interest.

"You wouldn't believe how my day went," I finally blurted out.

"Tell me about it," she asked as a good wife. "Maybe I will believe it!"

"Well, I have been told the following by several different people. Some one said we must go to elder rule or he will leave the church. Some one else said that if we do to elder rule, it will ruin the church."

Her mouth dropped open and an unbelieving smile came on her face. I continued.

"Some one else said that congregational rule is to allow the monkeys to run the zoo, or it is like letting the inmates govern the penitentiary, or to let the babies run the nursery. This one was convinced that I must take charge of the church and lead it with authority like a mafia leader---he even offered to be my intimidator."

She interrupted me with her laughter, recognizing those statements had to come from Dink.

I continued.

"Some one else said elder rule cannot possibly be right because it would be dictatorship and would thus ruin the church. This one assured me elder rule cannot be right because each of us has the Holy Spirit to guide us in Christian living---we don't need elders to interfere in our lives. Besides, this one said, we would violate the priesthood of the believer if we went to elder rule."

"Whoa," Terry interrupted again. "I've heard enough. You were right---I don't believe you!" she stated kiddingly.

We discussed the matter further as we ate supper. Then having no evening responsibilities, I stretched out on the couch for awhile to do some toes-up meditation. As I mulled over this whole problem of church government, I came to some conclusions.

No church government could be effective without spiritual people and leaders.

Unspiritual people in a congregational government would lead to unbiblical decisions as to the life and ministry of the church. Obviously, this would corrupt the church in life, practice and ministry.

On the other hand, unspiritual people in an elder-led church would not follow the guidance and leadership of the elders even if the elders were spiritual. Rebellion would follow as the children of Israel rebelled against Moses.

Again, unspiritual leaders in a congregationally governed church or in an elder led church would never lead the church in the proper manner in doctrine, life, worship, ministry or discipline.

This was not to say any form of church government would be acceptable, but that even if we had the Biblical form, it could not function without spiritual people and spiritual leaders.

Thus, the primary goal must not be the establishment of a Biblical government, but to develop a spiritual congregation from which we could draw spiritual leaders to lead spiritual people. What a great danger, that we would have the correct form of government, but lack the greater need of a spiritual people to implement and carry it to its end of glorifying God in the government of His church.

Thus, it would do little good to move an unspiritual body from congregational rule to elder rule. We must never understand elder rule as some magic panacea which would suddenly turn an unspiritual church into a spiritual church and solve all its problems.

Therefore, governmental structure of the church was not to be our major goal. Rather, a spiritual body must be our primary goal or nothing else would be right in the church--- its worship, its program, its ministry, its evangelism, its missions program, its discipline, or its government.

To move an unspiritual body of people from congregational rule to elder led government would accomplish nothing positive, but it could bring a multitude of negatives.

I then began to ask a more important question---are we a spiritual people at Unity Baptist Church? Are we a spiritual people who are capable of serving God and governing His church if we did have the correct form of government? Or are we an unspiritual people who would abuse the Biblical form of government, whatever that form might be, if we had it?

I remembered the phrase from some reading which said, "No holiness, no heaven." I borrowed that idea in my thinking to conclude, "No godliness, no government." No form of government would bring the church to God's intended end and purpose without godliness in the members and leaders. That was not to conclude that any form of government is acceptable if God's people are godly. Surely a godly people will want God's way in every matter, including government.

Thus, my task now was to emphasize godliness to the people as we sought to understand the Biblical form of government.

The next thing I knew Terry was waking me so I could go to bed to think further during my real night slumbers.

8

Is Congregational Rule Biblical....?

Why is it that when the Lord begins to work on you concerning an issue, He seems to open the flood gates to saturate you completely on the matter? At least, that is the way I felt as this subject of church government began to unfold. I felt I was in the path of an avalanche which I could not possibly dodge or evade in any way.

My next encounter on the subject came in a very unexpected manner. Due to no desire of my own, I had to stop by our local denominational office to pick up something for one of my members. Upon walking in the front door, I was met by Dr. Frakes, who was a pastor and also the moderator of our association. To my surprise he was unusually friendly towards me.

"Brother Ira, it sure is good to see you today. How's that new church?"

"Just fine," I replied, trying to hide my surprise.

"Brother Ira, have you got a minute? I need to talk to you about something," he continued in his warm and friendly manner. And though I really did not have time, I didn't want to appear to be unfriendly, so I told him I could take a few minutes to chat with him.

"Brother Ira, there's something going on in our association that I want to warn you about," he stated with seeming great concern.

With that statement he certainly piqued my curiosity, but I tried not to act too excited about the matter. I had been told he was something of a manipulator, and I especially remembered how he had been one of those in favor of the association censuring me for my doctrinal beliefs and the situation which had unfolded at First Baptist Church.

"Are you aware, Brother Ira, of a movement afoot in our association in some of our churches to lead them from congregational rule to elder rule?" he asked.

I gestured by giving a non-committal nod which said neither yes or no, but he didn't seem to care what my reply was or could have been as he continued with great emotion and fervor.

"Yes, there's a young man from an association to the north of us who is going around preaching in some of our churches that congregational rule is not Scriptural and that elder rule should be adopted by every church!"

He gave the young man's name, and it was Billy Motley, and then he set forth some negative remarks about him. This was all preparation for a very direct question to me.

"Brother Ira, you're solid on congregational rule, aren't you? You are convinced of its Biblical basis, are you not? No one could ever influence you or your church to move to elder rule, could they? We can count on you to help uphold the Baptist doctrine, can't we?"

Much to his dismay, I did not give him the answer he wanted, as I told him I was open to whatever the Bible taught on this as well as any subject. Evidently, he thought I was in danger of slipping away from his conviction, and he began to scold me and admonish me not to leave the historic Baptist position, which he said was the Biblical position. When he continued for several minutes, thinking he was waxing eloquent with powerful persuasion, I interrupted him with a statement and then a question.

"Brother Frakes, I am glad you brought that subject up, as we have run into the problem, and I have been looking for some answers. I would be ever so grateful if you could and would give me the Biblical arguments and evidence for congregational rule. I have looked for a solid Biblical exposition on the subject, but have not found it. I am open to hear your presentation, and would appreciate it very much."

With some apology and excuse that he did not have time just now, and that he would want to refer to his notes on the subject, he invited me to come to his church soon and we could spend as much time as needed to discuss the matter.

I understood that request, and to be honest appreciated it, since I had matters which needed my attention now as well. I also understood a need for him to study the matter so he could present the subject in its best argumentation.

As I left the associational office, I began to browse the New Testament from what knowledge I had stored in my memory, wondering which verses he would use for his position. I thought of a couple, but honestly, I could not think of very many. I really hoped he would do a good job in presenting the case for congregational rule. I did want to know the arguments and Biblical evidence for that view point.

I began to wish that God in His providence would have led Paul to write a divinely-inspired theology book. Honestly, I was looking forward to the next day and the arguments for congregational rule. I hoped he could think of more arguments for that position that I could on the spur of the moment, and that they would be Biblical.

9

Is That the Evidence....?

I didn't know quite what to expect the next day as I arrived at Dr. Frakes' office. Would I get a solid presentation and exposition of the Biblical evidence, or would I be given a shallow set of pragmatic and emotional arguments? And how would I react if I got the latter?

After the normal greetings and salutations, we sat down for our study. He was extra-friendly again, and appeared to be very confident in his attitude. He began the discussion with a rather lengthy statement.

"Before we turn to the Bible to discuss what it teaches, let me say that there are many arguments for congregational government in a local church. It is Baptistic! It is based on our view of the church! It is demanded by our view of the priesthood of the believer! It is one of the convictions which sets Baptists off from all others!"

I continued to listen, thinking we would soon turn to the Bible and seek to settle the issue there, but he continued.

"Plus congregational rule gives life and vitality to the church which no other governmental system can, for you see, it involves every member in the decision-making activity of the church. Who would want to be a member of a church where other people made decisions for you and simply dictated to each member the necessary actions without the individual having any voice in that decision?"

I was interested in what he was saying, but was still wondering when we would get to the Scriptures. I had no problem with a preface to the discussion, but wondered why all the talk before getting to our final authority.

"I think," he continued, "that many Baptists do not know the great genius of congregational rule, and that is why some are open to be deceived concerning elder rule. Is there any thing more beautiful than each member of the church participating in the church vote at a business meeting? Is there anything more exciting than a church voting to receive a new member, which gives him or her the right then to participate in all the decision-making actions of the church? Surely regenerated members have the Holy Spirit within them to enable them to think clearly about the life and ministry of the church, and then to cast their votes as He leads them."

I didn't want to look bored, but I was beginning to be bored! Maybe I should look bored so he would move on to the Biblical arguments, but I concluded he probably wouldn't even notice my boredom because he was on a roll and seemed to be enjoying it.

"After all," he continued, "Baptists believe that Jesus Christ is head of the church, and He will surely guide His church in the decision-making process. Is it not probably that the mind of God can be found more through the body making the decisions, than if just one individual or a group of individuals makes them?"

I was about to bite my tongue off to keep from saying something. Where was the Scriptural evidence? Why can't we look at Scripture, rather than talk in general concepts, which may or may not be found in Scripture? If I thought he was finished, I was sadly mistaken.

"One of the strongest objections to congregational rule is that it allows all members to vote, even the young people of the membership. So many feel they lack experience to be able to make the correct decisions, but again we must trust the same Holy Spirit who lives in us to lead them, even though they are babes in Christ. After all, Jesus said to be careful that we do not offend these young ones, and that it would be better for a millstone to be tied around our neck than we should offend even one of them."

I was fearful steam might very soon begin rising from my collar, because I was getting hot. Like in some of the other doctrinal pursuits I had made, men so often do not want to search the Scripture. They evade Scripture for emotional arguments, and even when they refer to Scripture, they do as he had done---pull a passage entirely out of its context and misapply it for the sake of their argument. I finally had to speak!

"Brother Frakes, would it be possible for us to come to the consideration of some passages of Scripture which bear directly on the subject? I realize you are trying to ground your case on other arguments, but my authority is the Bible, and that is what will settle it."

I had wanted to point out to him also that his "young people" who he thought should be allowed to vote, have at times in Baptist churches been children, even of a very tender age. I decided against this action, so I might give him opportunity to present his whole case. I was not there to argue with him, but to hear his arguments.

His answer was a little tense as he said, "Well, I am coming to that, but let me finish these other considerations. As I was saying, in a Baptist church each member is equal, regardless of background, education, age, or any other consideration. Thus, each member must have all the same rights of membership and an equal voice in the life of the church. And even if the church makes some wrong decisions, we must trust the Lord to bring good from this, as He is the Lord of His church!"

I was in a blur now! Much talk, but what had he said that was based on Scripture? I tried to summarize what he had said in my mind, but found I could not---it all seemed to fuzz together. I was certain of one thing---he had not offered any valid Scriptural evidence thus far. He had only given high-sounding platitudes and ungrounded principles. Maybe they were in the Bible, but he had yet to ground his argument on the authority of the Word of God.

He paused, perhaps sensing my frustration, and made a friendly gesture. "Can I get you something to drink---a Coke or Pepsi or whatever?"

I thanked him, but declined.

I hastened to ask, "Is that the strongest evidence you have for congregational rule? I am concerned that we have been talking for so long [actually he had been talking], and we have not mentioned one verse of Scripture which speaks directly to the issue."

I was going to say more, but his face dropped, and he seemed to lose the friendly edge and peppy attitude. I was almost sorry I had asked him the question, if that was the strongest evidence he had for congregational rule. I was beginning to wonder if such arguments existed!

Finally the Bible....!

It does not build confidence in the man or the case he is advocating if he seems to skirt the use of Scripture. That seemed to be what Dr. Frakes was doing, until I pressed him to give me his Biblical evidence for congregational rule.

He picked up his Bible with some reluctance and began to address the issue.

"Well, the first passage I would use is Acts 6:1-9. Here it is clear that when the church needed deacons, they were told 'Look you out among you seven men.'"

He opened his Bible and pointed to Acts 6:3.

He continued, "That was a decision of the whole church. It was not the action of a select few or of just one individual. It was the action of the whole church. That is the way Baptists churches select deacons today, and the way they make all their decisions as well."

I had several questions, but did not raise them at this point. I wanted to see his arguments, and I also sensed he was not open to any challenge of his ideas.

When I did not interrupt him, he continued, but his attitude was testy and unsettled.

"Also, in Acts 10:47 we see the church making the decision concerning the receiving of candidates for baptism and church membership. Not even Peter made the decision to baptize and receive Cornelius and his household. He asked, 'Can any man forbid water, that these should not be baptized, who have received the Holy Spirit as well as we?" Thus, the whole congregation made the decision that these were qualified for church membership. True, this is an unusual situation for these were Gentiles. But even so, the church made the decision for them to be baptized and received into the local church."

I had some questions again, but recorded them in my notebook for later consideration, and I was glad I was also recording the session for future listening and reference. I nodded and indicated he could continue.

"Moving to another argument, we must note that Paul wrote his letters to the churches and not to the leaders. This surely indicates that the local church was the final authority and not just the leaders. He felt he needed to convince the entire membership of the truth because they were the ones who had to make the decisions for the church. If the leaders only were the ones ruling the church, he would have addressed only them. Note such a passage as Romans 1:7, which says, 'To all that be in Rome, beloved of God, called to be saints.' Surely the word 'all' indicates the authority to make the decisions rested in the entire membership."

I did note to myself that this was not a strong argument. In fact, it was a weak one. I indicated by another nod for him to continue. I hoped he didn't take the nod as an indication that I agreed with him.

"Next, we consider I Peter 2:9. This text refers to a local church, and it states (in the plural), '...ye are a chosen generation, a royal priesthood, an holy nation, a peculiar people; that ye should show forth the praises of him who hath called you out of darkness into his marvelous light.' Do we not see the doctrine of the priesthood of the believer here---the local church is a royal priesthood? Surely every member of the body is important, and thus are capable of helping to make the decisions of the church. No one is excluded!"

I fought hard again not to raise questions on this one. What a poor handling of Scripture. He had made it say what he wanted it to say from the one word, 'priesthood,' and then he had jumped some premises never shown to conclude that it taught congregational rule. He continued this time even before I nodded.

"Now I know you are going to ask me about the matter of elders in the churches. It is clear, according to verses such as Titus 1:5, where it speaks of appointing elders in the churches, that the church is the one who appointed them. A.T. Robertson, the great Baptist Greek scholar, says the Greek word for 'appoint' means 'to vote by a showing of hands.' Thus from the basis of understanding of this great Greek scholar, the elders were not the final authority in the church, but the church was, for it was the church which voted on the elders, and thus they must have voted on other matters as well."

I couldn't resist a question, so I asked humbly, "Could you tell me what Greek word we are referencing here?"

He answered, "No, I didn't write it down, but you can find it in the Greek New Testament or in Robertson's writings."

I had to ask another question, as I queried, yet not wishing to offend.

"Could you give me a reference in A.T. Robertson's writings for that quotation?"

Again he looked a little sheepish as he admitted he was not sure where the reference was located. I had to wonder if he had done the research for himself or if he was just quoting someone else. And if Robertson had said that, did he also draw the same conclusion of congregational rule. Dr. Frakes' method did not encourage my heart that he had practiced careful study nor scholarship.

In fact, the whole case did not appear to be careful scholarship. It appeared to be more of a collection of a few verses which were used to draw his own conclusions. Careful Biblical interpretation was in question. Plus, what about all the other verses on elders. He had used only one, which he thought could teach congregational rule.

I almost felt I could have presented a better case for congregational rule than he had. I decided I could not judge the case on such weak arguments of one who had not done his homework. I wondered as I drove away if this session had proven anything. I decided it did prove one of two things: either congregational rule has a weak case, or the case I had heard had come from a weak source.

My search was just beginning!

11

Softball Theology....?

The rest of the day was spent in pastoral duties---hospital visitation and other sick calls. I was glad I had recorded my sessions with Dr. Frakes, and would be able to listen to it again.

That evening (about 5:30) I headed out to our church softball game. I wasn't too excited about church softball, since our experiences at First Baptist Church. I had seen too many ungodly actions during church sports events, as there seemed to be something about them that brought out the flesh in players. Plus, some teams didn't play by the eligibility rules. Players were supposed to attend so many services a month, but some stacked their teams with ringers, who never set foot in the church---all in the name of winning games as the ultimate goal.

Plus, many times there was tension on our own team as to who should play what position and when. We always had more players than the needed ten, and there was no way every one could start the game. Sometimes players never got in the game, depending on the difficulty of the opponent. Then if substitutions were made, the men coming out weren't exactly happy.

I told the coach I would be glad to just watch, but he insisted on playing me, and at a position I didn't even want to fill---pitcher and in a fast-pitch league. In our first few games several guys tried to pitch, but they couldn't get the ball over the plate, which resulted in the fielders standing idle while men walked around the base paths, knowing they didn't even need to swing at the ball.

One day the coach asked me if I had ever pitched. I couldn't lie to him, so I had to tell him I had pitched a little when I was in the eighth grade. He inserted me into the line-up to pitch the next game (to everyone's surprise and over my firm objections), and we won the game.

He then informed me to be ready to pitch each game in the weeks to come. He laughed as he told me saying, "You're not the greatest pitcher I have ever seen. You do have three speeds---slow, slower and slowest. But you do get the ball over the plate, and when they hit it we can try to chase it down in the field, and hope to get someone out. And when we come to bat, we can try to outscore them from the previous inning.

And he wasn't the only one who laughed at my lack of speed---the whole team did. It wasn't that my pitches had a big arc on them like in slow-pitch softball. No, my pitches came in over the plate without the arc, but any slower and they would have been arcing.

This evening, after my meeting with Dr. Frakes, I watched as our coach maneuvered our players, making his moves, substituting one for another, calling for bunts and steals. And then a thought came to my mind.

What if we had to take a vote of the church softball team on every move our coach made---before he made it? Who does the team want to start as pitcher? at catcher?, etc. Shall we bunt on this pitch? Shall I substitute Bill the best defensive outfielder in the late innings for Sam the better hitter?

Someone had to be in charge of a softball team. It could not be a congregationally run outfit. That would breed great confusion and chaos. In fact, this was true of every organization---someone had to be in charge.

I reminded myself that a church was not a softball team, and that the Bible had to be the final authority concerning the government of a church. I also re-established in my thinking that even if the Biblical church government did not make sense to me, nor agree with the world and its way of doing things, my conscience was bound to the Word of God, and I must obey its teachings on the subject.

We won the game that night, and as I drove home, I recalled all the wise moves our coach had made throughout the game that enabled us to win. I remembered too some of the grumbling on the bench, when he pulled certain players, and inserted others at one point in the game. I remembered I had been especially fearful when he stuck with me on the mound when they loaded the bases with two out in the last inning. When he visited me before I pitched to the last batter, I almost insisted he take me out. I wanted to win the game, but I did not want to disappoint the team.

As it turned out, the last batter drove the ball deep into left field. When it left his bat, I just knew it was out of the park. But Bill, our left fielder, the player who had been inserted in that inning for defensive purposes (he was a great fielder but didn't hit much), made a leaping catch against the fence, and we won the game.

As I savored the win and the thrill of victory on the way home with Terry, and as we discussed all the decisions our coach had to make during the game, Terry had a jewel of a comment.

"Aren't you glad your softball team isn't governed like the average Baptist church?"

12

Were Those Good Arguments....?

The next day as I sat in my office trying to work on my Sunday sermon, I found it difficult to concentrate. My mind was on the arguments I had heard for congregational rule. I decided to get the tape of our session and try to summarize those arguments.

As I listened, I took notes, stopping and starting the recorder as needed, in order to be sure I got the arguments with clarity. When I was finished, I had divided Dr. Frakes' arguments into two kinds---Scriptural and non-Scriptural ones. I noted them as follows:

1. Non-Scriptural arguments for congregational rule

    a. It is Baptistic.

    b. It is based on the Baptist view of the church.

    c. It is demanded by the Baptist doctrine of the priesthood of the believer.

    d. It is a conviction that sets Baptists off from all others.

    e. It gives life and vitality to the church as it involves every member.

    f.   It is something beautiful and exciting.

    g.   It is strengthened by the doctrine of the Holy Spirit as He guides the church.

    h.   It is indicated by the idea that more minds are better in decision-making than one.

    i.   It keeps us from offending the younger members.

    j.   It rests on the understanding that every member is equal.

    k.   It must be an act of faith, trusting that if the church makes a wrong decision, the Lord of the church will bring good from it.

    l.   It is proven by the fact that Jesus Christ is the head of His church.

2. <u>Scriptural grounds for congregational rule</u>

    a.   Acts 6:1-9---the early church not the elders chose the first deacons.

    b.   Acts 10:47---the church voted whether to baptize the converts at the home of Cornelius.

    c.   I Peter 2:9---the church is called a royal priesthood.

    d.   Titus 1:5---Paul left Titus at Crete to appoint
         elders in every city. The great Greek scholar
         A.T. Robertson says this Greek word means
         to vote by a show of hands.

In analyzing these arguments, I came to realize that some of them had to be considered, while others could be quickly dismissed. But before I could even make these distinctions, I had to be sure I had a correct understanding of each argument.

But that presented a problem. Dr. Frakes had not fully stated them, but had only set them forth in a sentence or two. I had to try to fill in the blanks in his thinking. I decided to take them one by one and try to do that, and only then render a judgment on the arguments.

1a. Congregational government is Baptistic.

I concluded that this is not a real argument for it assumes a premise---that is, that something Baptistic is right. The argument went as follows: Anything Baptistic is right. Congregational rule is Baptistic. Therefore we must conclude that congregational rule is right This argument could only convince the person who assumed being Baptistic is the goal of the church, rather than being Biblical.

2a. Congregational government is based on the Baptist view of the church.

The problem with this argument is the same as 1a---it assumes a premise. The argument is as follows: The view of church government based on the Baptist view of the church is correct. Congregational rule is based on the Baptist view of the church. Therefore, congregational rule is the correct view. Before one could use this argument, he would have to prove that the Baptist view of the church was Biblical. And before one could do that, he would have to state what is meant by the Baptist view of the church.

Recalling the reading I had done in Baptist history, I concluded (since Dr. Frakes had not stated it) that the Baptist view of the church intended here is the concept of a voluntary membership. That is, one is not a candidate for church membership until that one is capable of a voluntary personal profession of faith in Christ, accompanied by a commitment to unite with the local manifestation of the body of Christ, that is, the local church.

Even assuming that was the Baptist view of the church intended by Dr. Frakes, I could not see how such a conviction concerning voluntary membership in a local church necessarily brought the conclusion of congregational rule in the church. Not only would one have to assume the basic premise in this argument, but he would also have to jump a few others to reach the final conclusion. Therefore, I had to rule this to be a false argument for congregational rule as well.

1c. <u>Congregational rule is demanded by the Baptist doctrine of the priesthood of the believer</u>.

The first step in analyzing this argument was to define the much used but seldom defined term "priesthood of the believer." I had heard the term before, but usually by someone who wanted to state his freedom to allow Baptists to believe any thing they desired and still call themselves Baptists.

I summarized the term "priesthood of the believer" as follows: that every believer is a priest before God and has no need of any human priest or priesthood to represent him before God; that Christ is our great high priest who represents us at the throne of God in heaven; that Christ is the fulfillment of the Old Testament system of priesthood, and because of Him all such earthly systems of priests have passed away.

The conclusion from this definition seemed to be that if it is impossible for someone to represent a man before God, then it is also impossible for one to dictate convictions and beliefs to another man's conscience, since he is a priest before God and capable of interpreting the Bible for himself.

The relation of all this to church government is the conclusion that since each man is a priest before God with no human representation at the throne of God, then each man also should be able to express that freedom and relationship in the life and government of the local church without anyone standing between him and God in the decision-making of the church.

To state it another way, because each member is equal before God, then each member also has an equal voice in the life of the church and government. Thus, one can only conclude congregational rule. All men in the church are equal before God and therefore equal before one another and therefore equal in voice in the government of the church.

I concluded that if this was the argument, it was somewhat stronger than the first two, yet it could not be a primary argument for congregational rule. The verses dealing more directly with church government must set the position, and then this argument must be weighed in light of those conclusions. Or in other words, this argument could not become the hermeneutical tool to determine the doctrine of the government of the church. It would only be determined as valid or invalid when considered with the rest of the Biblical data on the church and its leaders and its government.

About this time, as I was deeply engrossed in my pursuit, old Todd wandered into the office.

"What's up, Doc?" he chided as he spread himself out in one of my chairs.

"Well, not much more than study!" I answered. "How's your study on church government going?" I cautiously asked.

"Oh, we're voting Wednesday evening to go to elder rule!?" he smilingly and proudly stated.

"This Wednesday?" I asked with a dumfounded look and voice.

"Yup, this Wednesday!" he repeated with a greater air of joy and confidence. "Come Thursday morning, we will be the first church in our association to have elder rule."

To be honest, I wasn't sure of that statement.

13

We'll Be the First....!

To be honest, I couldn't see what was the great accomplishment of being first to adopt elder rule in the association. In fact, it left me a little upset with Todd's shallowness. I had to ask some questions.

"Well, what have you done to prepare for this switch?" I began to feel like I was conducting an inquisition.

"Oh, I preached on it a couple of times," he remarked rather matter-of-factly.

"And how did it go?" I asked.

"Well, I guess it went all right?" he said with some air of unconcern.

"You guess it went all right?" I queried. "And you are still going to bring it to a vote with such uncertainty?"

I couldn't resist burning him with another question, even if it embarrassed him.

"Todd, give me the strongest argument for elder rule and the strongest argument for congregational rule."

"Oh, come on, Ira! You know you're into these things deeper than I am. No matter what I say, you will play the devil's advocate and tear me up. I'm sure glad I'm dealing with uneducated people who don't think too deeply on these matters, so that I can convince them with the arguments I give. We don't over-analyze these things at Lime Creek. We just seek to follow the Bible!"

I could tell he was getting upset, so I backed off. I only said, "Todd I hope the Lord doesn't have to teach you a very costly lesson concerning the need to be a more serious student of the Word and a more patient leader of His church. I would never bring a matter to my church until I and they understood the issues, and therefore, we could make an intelligent decision based on the best study of the Scriptures."

When he saw I had backed off, he flashed his silly grin and fired back boldly, "This will be their last vote! And it will be a vote to eliminate future voting forever and turn the church over to the leadership of the elders."

I couldn't resist one final thrust.

"What if they vote to continue to vote, thus not making this their final vote, and then vote to vote you out?"

With that he exited muttering he wasn't worried about that, and that he was going to play some golf.

By this time I was tired of weak arguments for congregational rule, and the weak discipline of one who was advocating elder rule but was unwilling to study the issue in depth. I discovered that I was even more determined to find the truth concerning the issue of church government. I determined to plow through a few more of the arguments of congregational rule, as difficult as it was.

1d. <u>Congregational rule is a conviction that sets Baptists off from all other denominations</u>.

This argument also was obviously weak and even fallacious. The argument actually was saying that something is correct because it is different from all other views on the subject. It should be clear to any one that just because one position is different from all others does not make it the correct view. Suppose you had four positions and they were all different from each other. Which one would be true, according to this standard?

1e. <u>Congregational rule gives life and vitality to the church as it involves every member in the life and decisions of the church.</u>

Again, this is a fallacious argument. It may be true that congregational rule gives life and vitality to the church. It may be true that it involves every member in the life and decisions of the church. But does that prove it is the correct government of the church? Not hardly.

On that pragmatic basis of thinking, any thing which gives vitality to the church would be a correct practice. Any thing which would involve every member in the life and decision of the church would be a correct practice. Clearly this premise could lead to some dangerous and unscriptural practices. And where is the Bible in this argument?

1f. <u>Congregational rule is something beautiful and exciting.</u>

Again, this is a false argument based on a dangerous premise. Any thing that is deemed "beautiful and exciting" is legitimized in the life and practice of the church.

1g. <u>Congregational rule is strengthened by the doctrine of of the Holy Spirit, in that He guides the church.</u>

Again, this is a fallacious argument. There is not a clarity concerning what is meant by the idea that the Holy Spirit is the guide of the church. The real question is not whether the Holy Spirit guides the church or not, but the question is, how does the Spirit guide the church---through congregational rule or elder leadership? That is the issue which must be decided by Scripture, not by emotional arguments.

1h. <u>Congregational rule is indicated by the idea that more minds are better than one</u>.

Again this argument is weak and unconvincing. The premise that more minds are better than one is proven in the argument neither by Scripture nor by logic.

1i. <u>Congregational rule keeps us from offending the younger members</u>.

Dr. Frakes had quoted in this argument Matthew 18:6. That verse reads, "But whosoever shall offend one of these little ones who believes in me, it were better for him that a millstone were hanged about his neck, and that he were drowned in the depth of the sea."

The argument seems to be that to do anything that offends a younger believer (some how in Dr. Frakes' argument the younger believer becomes a young member of the church) is a very serious matter and will bring severe consequences. Dr. Frakes, as he used this verse for argument, gave no context to narrow the meaning of the verse, but simply applied it to his conviction of congregational rule. The idea seems to be that the verse can be applied to anything in the life of the church which might offend a young believer. Surely the context needs to be considered.

Actually the context of Matthew 18 is the receiving of a young believer, not the authorization of this young believer to vote in the decision-making process of the church. There is no indication that refusing to let a young believer vote is in the mind of the author. Thus, this too is a weak argument.

I was worn out now by these fallacious, non-biblical arguments. I was eager to get to the Biblical ones. Therefore I was not too upset when the phone rang. But I soon realized I would have to keep thinking about church government for it was Mrs. Palmer. I had asked her to find the arguments for congregational rule.

"Pastor Pointer, I have been studying this matter of church government just as you asked me to do. I have found the best speaker who could come and address our church on the subject. I have just come from talking to him, and he is absolutely persuasive on this subject. I know he will convince us all, including you, Pastor, if we could just invite him to speak to us. After all, we had a speaker on the side of elder rule, and now surely we need to hear one from the other side of the argument."

I must admit I was encouraged by her interest and glad to know she had found a good representative   of congregational rule.

Eagerly I asked, "Who is it you have found?"

My heart dropped as she said, "Dr. Frakes of Longwood Baptist Church."

14

More Arguments....!

I was caught off guard by Mrs. Palmer's suggestion of Dr. Frakes to speak to us on congregational rule. What was I to say to her suggestion, when he was the one giving me such weak arguments on the subject? Evidently his weak arguments had convinced her!

"Mrs. Palmer," I began slowly. "I thank you for your suggestion, and I do want to be open to hear all arguments, but I have already heard Dr. Frakes' position on the matter." I went on to explain how I had encountered him at the associational office, and how he had been willing to give me his arguments on the subject. I did not have the heart to tell her I thought his presentation was very weak, but I had to tell her something and remain in the realm of honesty.

"I have tried to analyze his arguments, and I really don't think they are the strongest that one could give for congregational rule. Could I ask you to keep looking for the arguments? Or maybe you could summarize his arguments for me?"

She thanked me, and promised she would keep pursuing the subject and would be in touch.

When I finally got off the phone, it was time to head home for supper. I piled my Greek books into my briefcase with hopes I would get some opportunity that evening to consider some of the remaining arguments Dr. Frakes had given.

As I drove home I propped the final non-biblical arguments up on my dashboard, being careful not to be distracted to the point of making some driving error. I concluded that the last three arguments were no stronger than the others. Therefore, why should I spend any more time on them? They were all divorced from any reference to Scripture. Thus, I gave them all a dismissal with just a few mental comments.

1j. <u>Congregational rule rests on the understanding that every member is equal</u>.

Where is the Scripture that states every member is equal? And equal in what? Such lack of clarity of definition does not establish clarity in the desired conclusion.

1k. <u>Congregational rule must be an act of faith, trusting that if the church makes the wrong decision, the Lord of the church will bring good from it</u>.

I concluded that this point is not an argument in favor of congregational rule, but a statement of how this system of government corrects the possibility of mistakes it may generate.

1l. <u>Congregational rule is proven by the fact that Jesus Christ is the head of the church</u>.

There is no question about it---Jesus Christ is head of the church. But what does that statement really prove? Why does it prove congregational rule? Why couldn't it prove there is no need of any government in the church--- just let Jesus rule. Again, the final argument is weak as it states a Scriptural premise, but fails to establish any truthful premises which would lead to the conclusion of congregational rule.

Suddenly my preoccupation of thought was joltingly disturbed as I was aware of the flashing light of a police car in my rear view mirror. I wondered what stupid thing I had done while engrossed in my subject of thought.

I slowed down, and the police car swung up beside me. It was Troy Medford, one of my church members. He signaled for me to follow him, and now I was concerned. Did he want to stop me for fellowship or for a traffic violation? It was always a joy to fellowship with him as he was a very young officer, and a new convert in Christ. He was growing so fast I could hardly keep up with him.

I followed him into Handy Andy's and he jumped out and asked me if I had time for a Coke. Reading in his face that something was bothering him, and giving a sigh of relief that I had not broken some law, I agreed. After calling my wife to tell her I would be late for supper, I sat down across from him in one of the booths in Handy's.

I noted, as we said hello, that something very serious was on his mind. He spoke rather matter-of-factly, not even waiting for me to ask any questions.

"Some one is trying to kill me!"

My immediate reaction was, "What...? Who?"

"I wish I knew," he stated shaking his head.

Then something happened that I am not sure I could even describe in full details now.

All of a sudden he dove across the table, hit me with a body block, and sent me sprawling to the floor. At the same time I felt a sharp pain pierce my body. I thought I had hit some sharp object in the fall, until I reached up to touch my left shoulder and discovered blood oozing out.

"They got you, Ira!" Troy yelled as he pulled his revolver and crawled towards the door.

"Stay down!" he barked in his authoritative police voice.

Really, he had nothing to worry about. I wasn't about to raise my head. In fact, even in the midst of the pain, I managed to crawl further under the table for greater shelter. I began to feel woozy, like I was going to pass out.

As I drifted into la-la land, I light-headedly and somewhat humorously asked myself if I had under-estimated the seriousness of my present pursuit on the subject of church government. I wondered if I had stirred up some one who was willing to kill for it! I laughed as I surrendered myself to the wooziness and over-powering weakness of my body.

I remember asking myself why I was not afraid in light of the fact I might be dying.

I also remember thinking, along with the above thought, and again with some humor, that maybe I will have this question of church government answered by the highest divine authority---at the feet of Jesus. He would surely know the answer!

15

Who Is Trying to Kill Me....?

When one rises on any given day, he never knows what that day may bring. Only a fool would think he has some absolute guarantee of rising the next day. If one thinks of any unexpected tragedy, he must realize that none of the persons involved expected to leave the world that day, unless, of course, he was going to be the purposeful author of the tragedy.

The last thing I would ever have thought at the beginning of this certain day was that I would be shot by a gun before the day was finished.

I do know that my first thought when I woke up in the hospital was, "Who in the world is trying to kill me?" My second thought concerned how badly I was hurt. My third thought was a question, and a rather stupid one---"How long will this stall my study on the subject of church government?"

The answer to the first question, concerning who was trying to kill me, was that no one was trying to turn me into a cold corpse. Whoever had shot, so I was told by my police officer friend, was not trying to kill me. They were aiming at him. That is what he was trying to tell me when I was shot. I still needed to talk to him about this matter. I was really concerned for him. If they had been so bold as to accost us in broad daylight in Handy's, I was really concerned about his safety. I was dripping with eagerness to know what was going on in this situation.

The answer to the second question was that I was not badly hurt, but had taken a bullet in the left shoulder. It left me in some pain and in the hospital a few days, but I was assured I would recover without any permanent damage.

The answer to the third question was that I now had some time whereby I could pursue the subject while in the hospital, and then while idled at home for a few days. I gave my wife, Terry, instructions concerning which books to bring me, and between visits from nurses and friends, I dug into the subject again---with her willing help, of course.

I was glad I had finished the non-biblical arguments, so we could now turn to the Biblical ones. We began with Acts 6:1-9---what most people assume to be the election of the first deacons. I asked Terry to read the passage to me.

1 And in those days, when the number of the disciples was multiplied, there arose a murmuring of the Grecians against the Hebrews, because their widows were neglected in the daily ministration.
2 Then the twelve called the multitude of the disciples unto them, and said, It is not reason that we should leave the word of God, and serve tables.
3 Wherefore, brethren, look among you for seven men of honest report, full of the Holy Spirit and wisdom, whom we may appoint over this business.
4 But we will give ourselves continually to prayer, and to the ministry of the word.
5 And the saying pleased the whole multitude; and they chose Stephen, a man full of faith and of the Holy Spirit, and Philip, and Prochorus, and Nicanor, and

*Timon, and Parmenas, and Nocolas, a proselyte of
Antioch.
6 Whom they set before the apostles; and when they
had prayed, they laid their hands on them.
7 And the Word of God increased, and the number of
the disciples multiplied in Jerusalem greatly; and a
great company of the priests were obedient to the
faith.*

As we went back over the passage, we were amazed as
we noted the following:

1. If this is a deacon selection, then deacons were not
    originally chosen to be any kind of spiritual leaders
    in the church, but to be servants---to take care of
    the Grecian widows in the daily ministration. Simply
    stated, they were servants concerning material
    needs. They were selected to take care of these
    material needs so the apostles would not have to
    leave the ministry of the Word of God and prayer
    in order to do it.

2. It is true that the twelve instructed the multitude of
    the disciples (they called them to themselves---they
    did not go to these disciples), and they instructed
    them to "look among you for seven men of honest
    report, full of the Holy Spirit and wisdom." We
    noted several observations from this statement:

    a. This multitude of disciples, who were instructed
        to find the deacons, were called to the twelve.
        The question this statement had to raise was if
        this was really the whole church selecting the

deacons. If they had wanted the whole church involved in it, they would have needed to go to the whole church in one of its services. We concluded this could not be the whole church making a selection, as Dr. Frakes had argued. It had to be a representative group from the church or churches. Thus deacons were not selected by a vote of the "whole" church.

b. The qualifications for deacons was clearly set forth by the twelve. The deacons must be men who were full of the Holy Spirit and wisdom. This was not some popularity vote or choice. These men had to be spiritual men---that was the primary qualification.

c. These were men who were chosen---not women. The Greek word used here definitely speaks of the male gender.

3. The apostles were the ones who finally and actually "appointed" these seven when they were found by the representatives of the church or churches.

a. The apostles appointed them (verse 3). The Greek word for "appoint" means to place, to set, or to appoint. Thus, the apostles seemed to have a final approval. It does not say what the twelve would have done had they been presented with an unqualified person, but it seems clear if that had been the case, and they knew it, they never would have appointed such men to office.

      b.   The apostles not only appointed them, but they laid hands on them after they had prayed (verse 6). They were clearly set aside to the task for which they were being appointed.

After noting these thoughts (Terry who was serving as my scribe and adding her thoughts as we progressed), we were surprised at what we had seen in just this simple understanding of the passage. It did not say what Dr. Frakes claimed at all. We summarized our thoughts as follows:

1. The early deacons were not elected by a vote of the church.

2. The early deacons were selected by representatives of the church or churches (it must be remembered that this was in Jerusalem where thousands had been saved).

3. The early deacons met very clear qualifications--- they had to be full of the Holy Spirit and men of wisdom.

4. The early deacons were approved by the twelve in that they were the ones who set them aside to the ministry by "appointing them" and then by "laying hands on them."

5. The deacons were men and not women.

6. The early deacons were not authoritative or even spiritual leaders of the church, but they were servants taking care of the material needs of the widows of the congregation.

7. This passage clearly contradicts the claim of Dr. Frakes that this was the decision of the whole church.

I was excited about what we were seeing. We had not solved the puzzle yet, but we had unearthed one piece, and that was exciting.

Suddenly my excitement was interrupted by a sharp pain in my shoulder, and I was brought back to the remembrance and the reality of my injury.

Terry saw the look of pain, and said smilingly but firmly, "We'd better quit and you had better rest now---and we aren't going to vote on that either."

I took that as a clear statement she wasn't willing to continue to be my scribe, so I had no choice. An authoritative decision had been made in love, and I knew she was right in the decision. She knew me too well---I would have kept going even to my detriment.

As I drifted off to sleep, my mind came back to the question, who had tried to kill me (or Troy---as he insisted), and why? Who and why? I had no answers! Would the perpetrators try again soon?

I looked forward to discussing the matter very soon with Troy!

16

I Have All Kinds of Questions....!

When I woke up the next morning, I wondered if I was improving or regressing. Part of it was that it was Sunday, and I was out of my pulpit. As far as my physical condition was concerned, I was told that often that's the way it is--- you feel worse the next few days after an accident than when it happens. I surely hoped I would not have to spend very many days in such confinement, though I decided today was all right in light of the way I felt.

About mid-morning, as I was still trying to figure out how I really felt, Troy walked into the room. To be honest, he was the guy I wanted to see, even though I felt a little weak.

"How are you doing, Pastor?" he asked with an apparent concern.

I smiled and replied, "Not bad for a guy who took a bullet, then they wouldn't let him keep it."

He managed a smile in return, but it was apparent that he was still very concerned about something.

"Troy," I almost ordered him, "tell me what's going on. All I remember before being shot was that you said some one was trying to kill you."

I repeated the questions I had sputtered out when first told of the subject, just before I took the bullet.

"Who is trying to kill you , and why?"

"I wish I knew," he replied.

"You mean you have no idea?" I asked.

"Not really. If I did, I could investigate and see if my suspicions were true. But I haven't got the foggiest idea," he admitted. "Someone like me, a police officer who has arrested a lot of people, who has put a lot of people away, who has given a lot of tickets, has no way of knowing who might come after him---maybe some kook I don't even know or maybe a guy who hates policemen who has just picked me out randomly."

"Aren't you afraid?" I asked with some emphasis.

"Well, yes, but then I remember what you have taught me at church on the sovereignty of God. This guy, whoever he is, can't do anything to me that God does not allow! That's comforting. Yet I know that doesn't mean I don't try to find out who it is and bring him to justice. But the doctrine of God's sovereignty has become the foundation of my entire life---even my police work."

I must admit I was a little ashamed that I hadn't been encouraging him in that foundational doctrine at this moment, but I was glad my preaching was being applied in a very practical manner. And he had just preached me a sermon reminding me that this bullet, which had sought me out, was not some act of chance outside the will of God, but that it was part of His plan for my life.

"Well, what can I do to help you find this guy?" I asked, volunteering my services.

"Preacher, you just get well, and let us take care of this guy, whoever he is," he said as he gathered his cap and evidenced he was ready to go.

"Let me ask you one more question before you go," I boldly invited.

"Go ahead, but I haven't been very good at answering your questions today, have I?"

"Well, surely you can answer this one. Why did you throw a body-block against me just before the shot the other day in Handy Andy's? Did you see something? Did you see the guy who did it?"

"Yes, I saw a guy just outside the window, and I saw a gun come out of his pocket, and in light of the fact I had been fired on twice before, I figured it might be another attempt to get me. You were between me and the gunman, and I figured he might hit you, so I floored you. I hope I didn't hurt you too badly. I'm sorry, but I thought it was necessary."

I thanked him for the move, and then smiled, commenting that it might have been easier on me if the cop who decked me hadn't been a six foot four and two hundred and fifty pound former all-state offensive tackle.

He laughed, and it seemed to break the tension, as he said, "I can't do anything about the height, but maybe I can do something about the weight. But then I'd never want to be a little skinny guy like you."

"Like me?" I protested. "I'm almost six feet tall and weigh now almost two hundred pounds."

"Like I said," he repeated, "I wouldn't want to be a little skinny guy like you."

After we prayed, he left and I settled down to scrambled thoughts which were fusing in my brain---Baptist church government and cold bullets. I couldn't see where they had any thing in common, but there they were blending together in my thought patterns.

17

Tell Me about Cornelius....!

I spent Sunday resting, but looked forward to Monday so I could pursue Dr. Frakes' interpretation of the conversion of Cornelius. But I had to wait for Terry to come to the hospital, because I was still unable to work alone. Sure enough, she arrived as promised, and seemed as eager as I was to dig into our study. She read the section to us from Acts 10:44-48:

44   While Peter yet spoke these words, the Holy Spirit fell on all them who heard the word.
45   And they of the circumcision who believed were astonished, as many as came with Peter, because on the Gentiles also was poured out the gift of the Holy Spirit.
46   For they heard them speak with tongues and mag-nify God. Then answered Peter,
47   Can any man forbid water that these should not be baptized, who have received the Holy Spirit as well as we?
48   And he commanded them to be baptized in the name of the Lord. Then prayed they him to tarry certain days.

Dr. Frakes had argued that here we see the church making the decision concerning the receiving of candidates for baptism and church membership. He had said that not even Peter made the decision to baptize and receive Cornelius and his household. The whole congregation made the decision.

The key question concerns who Peter was addressing when he asked, "Can any man forbid water that these should not be baptized?"

We noted that Peter was not in his own home town with his local church. Neither was he in the setting of a local church in a foreign city. He was in Cornelius' home, a man who was not a Christian prior to Peter's visit.

Who then is it that Dr. Frakes says is voting here, if there is not the presence of a local church setting or service? The conclusion may very well be based on assumption, unless he can show the presence of a church, which could be voting as he claims.

Cornelius had called two household servants and a devout soldier and sent them to Joppa to get Peter (see verses 7-8). Peter was at Joppa, and others were with him (see verse 10). When God commanded and convinced Peter to go to Caeserea to Cornelius as requested, certain brethren accompanied him from Joppa (see verse 23). It seems clear that those accompanying him were Jews (see verses 28 and 45), while Cornelius was a Gentile (one of another nation---see verse 28).

Those Jews with Peter were astonished when Cornelius and his household were saved (verse 45). This is clearly stated in Scripture, and it is after this observation by the writer of Acts that Peter asks his question, "Can any man forbid water, that these should not be baptized who have received the Holy Spirit as well as we?"

Clearly, Peter was not calling for a vote of a local church so he could baptize these converts, but he was addressing a possible objection a Jew might have in a

Gentile being baptized. Peter had become convinced God would receive Gentiles, and now by a question, he was urging Jews with him to acknowledge the obvious---God had saved some Gentiles, and they are truly candidates for baptism---any objections? He was not getting their permission, but urging them to admit this was the will of God, which they did, for there were no objections.

We concluded that a careful consideration of the context did not confirm Dr. Frakes' position, but showed its weakness. Thus, Acts 10 did not teach congregational rule.

About the time we were finishing our study, old Todd walked into the room. I noticed that he didn't have his usual nothing-really-matters-to-me grin all over his face. He was rather solemn and serious.

After the usually pleasantries, as well as a question about my well-being, he blurted out his problem.

"They fired me last night, Ira! You were right---they fired me just like you said they would. I had wanted to bring it up next Wednesday night, but they called a special meeting last night and fired me straight out!"

He was about to cry, and as I looked closer through the dimmed light in the room, I could see had had been crying previously. I couldn't help feeling sorry for him, even though he had been so careless and over-confident when I had given him my warning.

I asked the obvious.

"Why did they fire you?"

"You know, Ira! You warned me. Why didn't I listen to you? Ira, why can't I be like you? I'm so impulsive and immature at times. Please help me!"

"Todd you're telling me that they not only rejected your plan for elder rule, but they also rejected your leadership as pastor?"

"That's about it! Boy did I goof! Now what am I going to do?"

He still hadn't told me much as he kept speaking in generalities. But as I kept probing, the following scenario came out.

When they called the special meeting, he presented elder rule to them without even running it through his deacons. He had preached it on Sunday morning and evening, and then unknown to him, they called the special meeting. He tried to defend himself at the meeting by reading a lengthy statement on the subject. He then called for a vote, hoping to head off a vote to fire him. Some did try to refer it to a committee, but Todd rejected that idea. Others tried to table the motion, but he stopped that also. He insisted they vote on the matter that night, and they did, and it failed.

The next move was to vote to dismiss him as pastor, and it carried by close to a one hundred per cent vote. Now he was sorry and acknowledging he had made a stupid move.

I noted to myself how quickly the bravado and false confidence of man can vanish when reality sets in. If only he had possessed the attitude he now possessed when we had talked a few day previously.

After we prayed, my heart still ached for him as he left. I told him I would pray further about some way I might be able to help him.

As he left, I thought to myself, the ministry can be cruel, but preachers can be stupid at times, too. Sometimes its hard to tell the one from the other. Some times the one leads to the other.

18

What Can I Do....?

I felt rather helpless lying in bed that night. I wanted to help catch a potential killer, and I wanted to help Todd, and I wanted to pursue my study subject of church government. And here I was confined for a few days, and then maybe there would be even more days and even weeks of a slower schedule.

About the time I was drifting off to sleep that Monday evening, the phone rang. It wasn't that the phone hadn't rung earlier in the day---it had. But now it was almost eleven o'clock and I was ready to go to sleep.

"Hello," I said rather sleepily.

"Is this Rev. Pointer?" a muffled harsh voice asked.

"Yes, it is," I replied, trying to figure out who it was.

"I want to apologize to you. The bullet wasn't meant for you. It was meant for your cop friend."

I would have sat straight up in the bed if my body could have taken the quick move. But mentally I came alive.

"Who is this?" I asked abruptly.

"Never mind! Just accept my apology for hitting you instead of him."

And then he was gone!

"Wait!" I called into the phone, but to no avail.

I settled back into the bed wide awake now. I began to think of the conclusions I could draw from this call.

First, Troy was right. I was not the target of the bullet.
Troy was, but they had gotten me accidentally, humanly
speaking.

Second, the assassin had a conscience, for why else
would he call to apologize to me?

Third, I could rest peacefully now. I had felt a little
uneasy in a dark quiet hospital room at night without the
normal activity of the day. It seemed to me it would have
been rather easy to finish the job if I was the target.

Fourth, I knew now I had to do all I could to protect
Troy. Somehow I had been brought into the situation, and
now I might be able to help Troy in some way.

I began to pray the hit man would call me back, and I
would have an opportunity not only to stop him from what
he intended to do, but even more---I wanted to share the
gospel with him.

The next morning the doctor gave me the news I could
go home if I would behave myself and not do anything for
about a week or so. Understandably, I agreed to his
restrictions, and home I went when Terry arrived.

After some rest and lunch and then more rest, we
decided we would take another step in our study. I decided
that the strongest argument left in Dr. Frakes' arsenal was
the Titus 1:5 passage, where he quoted A.T. Robertson, the
Greek scholar. As usual, Terry read the verse to us.

*For this cause I left thee in Crete, that thou shouldst
set in order the things which are wanting, and ordain
elders in every city as I had appointed thee.*

We reminded ourselves of Dr. Frakes' argument that
A.T. Robertson said that the Greek word for appoint means

"to vote by a showing of hands" We looked first at Robertson's comments on Titus 1:5, but we found nothing referring to voting by a show of hands. All he said was that the word for appoint "does not preclude the choice by the churches..." (ATR, Word Pictures, Vol. 4, p. 598)

He notes in this context that it is the same word used in Acts 6:3 for appoint. He says there that "the action of the apostles follows the choice by the church..." (ATR, Ibid., Vol. 3, p. 73)

Thus, in these two verses, though Robertson argues from the context for the church making its choice prior to the appointments by the apostles, he does not go as far as to say that the Greek word for appoint means "to vote by a show of hands." Thus, Dr. Frakes, or some one he read, took the Robertson statement and interpreted the word apart from the context. They took his final conclusion from the context and made it the definition of the word appoint. Such action is sloppy scholarship, and Robertson would not have agreed with such a handling of his statements.

Furthermore, we looked in all my Greek lexicons and not one of them defined the Greek word for appoint as "to vote by a show of hands." This pursuit included Liddel and Scott, Lampe's Patristic Greek Lexicon, Moulton and Milligen's Vocabulary of the Greek New Testament, Thayer's Greek lexicon, and the Arndt and Gingrich lexicon. Plus, we tracked down through Moulton and Geden's concordance to the Greek New Testament every use of the word used in Titus 1:5, and not in one place is it to be translated "to vote by a show of hands."

Terry and I could only shake our heads at such loose handling of the Scripture that one would make a word mean something which it does not mean as Dr. Frakes had done.

We couldn't be sure, but we concluded he probably had just misquoted or misread or misunderstood A.T. Robertson's arguments. Or he had quoted someone else who had misquoted or misread or misunderstood these arguments.

We had to admit that the case for congregational rule was looking weak, but we were not willing to embrace a position quite yet. There was much homework to be done concerning the argument for elder rule.

Then again, maybe we had not run across one who could defend and argue the congregational position in a strong way.

19

How Can I Help Todd....?

Our solemn and meditative evening was interrupted as always (so it seemed) by a phone call. It was Todd. He wanted to know if I had thought of anything he could do.

I asked him to come by the next day, and that I thought I had an idea which might help him. I wanted to think about it a little longer, but would share it with him tomorrow.

He agreed, and seemed relieved that I might help him.

I concluded its a lot easier to salvage a ministry before an explosion than after one.

Following Todd's call, I continued to pursue my study on church government. I was now ready to seek to understand what the Bible taught about elders, bishops, etc., and what place they played in the authority structure of the people of God in the Scriptures. I had decided to start in the Old Testament and move through the Bible concerning the subject.

I discovered that the Hebrew word for elder was zaqen. I was amazed to see the number of times the word was used in the Old Testament, not only concerning Israel (which was the primary usage), but also concerning the other nations, such as Egypt (see Genesis 50:7), Midian (see Numbers 22:4, 7), Moab (see Numbers 22:7), the Gibeonites (see Joshua 9:11), plus many other uses. The word was used to speak of those of elder age as well as those who were the leaders or rulers of the people.

Most impressive were the usages concerning God's people. It cannot be denied that God's people of the Old Testament times were led by elders. They were not a democracy. They were not governed by congregational rule. Some of the passages were as follows.

Ex 3:16---Moses was told to gather the elders of Israel

Ex 3:18---Moses and elders go before the king of Egypt

Ex 4:29---Moses and Aaron gather the elders

Ex 12:21---Moses called the elders of Israel and gave instructions for the Passover

Ex 17:5-6---Moses was to take the elders of Israel

Ex 18:12---the elders came to Moses and Joshua

Ex 19:7---Moses called for the elders of Israel

Ex 24:1---Moses and others and the elders were called up before God

Ex 24:9---Moses plus 70 elders and others to go up the mountain

Ex 24:14---the elders were to tarry

Lv 9:1---Moses called Aaron and the elders

Nu 11:16---the 70 elders were gathered

Nu 11:24---at Kadesh Barnea Moses gathers the 70 elders and the Spirit was given to them

Nu 11:25---the Spirit was given to the elders

Nu 11:30---Moses and the elders went into camp

Nu 16:25---Moses was followed to Dothan by the elders

Dt 19:12---the elders were given responsibility

Dt 21:2-3---the elders were given responsibility in cities

Dt 21:4---the elders were given responsibilities

Dt 21:6---the elders were acting

Dt 21:19-20---the elders were at the city gate ruling

Dt 22:15-18 (4 times)---the elders rule

Dt 27:1---Moses and the elders command the people
     to keep the commandments

Dt 31:9---Moses delivered the law to the elders

Dt 31:28---the elders were responsible for the people

Jos 7:6---Joshua and the elders grieve over Achan's sin

Jos 8:10---Joshua and the elders go before the people

Jos 8:33---the elders and Israel were at Ebal and
     Gerazim

Jos 23:2---Joshua called the people and elders for a last
     message

Jos 24;1---Joshua called the elders to Shechem

Jdg 2:7---the people served the Lord all the days of
     Joshua and the elders

Jdg 21:16---the elders made a decision

See also I Samuel 4:3, 8:4, 11:3, 15:30 and 30:26

See also II Samuel 3:17, 5:3, 17:4 and 17:15

See also I Kings 8:1, 8:3 and 20:7

See also I Chronicles 11:3, 15:25 and 21:16

See also II Chronicles 5:2 and 5:4

See also Psalms 105:22 and 107:32

See also Jeremiah 26:17, Ezekiel 7:26, 20:1 and 20:3

See also Ezra 5:5, 6:7, 6:8, 6:14, 10:8 and 10:14

From the above verses concerning the word "elder" in the Old Testament, as it is used both among Israel and the nations, we can draw the following conclusions:

1. The office of elder as a leader and ruler of the
    people was very common both among God's people
    and the nations in the Old Testament days.

2. The office of elder, though it is mentioned very extensively in the Old Testament, is not clearly defined regarding its qualification and duties.

3. The office of elder was in existence in Israel from the time of their slavery in Egypt and all through their history, including the post-exilic period.

My next study would have to wait for another time and would have to address the matter of elders among the Jews in the New Testament. Did the Jews continue elder leadership before the coming of Christ in the New Testament? Was there a change of method of leadership of God's people before then, or was there a change indicated in any place in the Christian community, understanding that the early Christians were Jews?

About this time, when we were ready to let our subject rest, the phone rang once again. Surprisingly it was Todd, and I could tell by the tone of his voice something had happened since I had talked to him previously.

"Ira, my good friend!" he greeted me with his old zip and enthusiasm. "Guess what?"

I had no idea of what to guess. I could only wonder if the church had in some manner changed its mind.

"I've got a job offer in another church!" he bragged.

"Where?" I queried searchingly.

"Middleville Baptist Church---in Middleville," he stated with a joyful air.

"Middleville?" I asked, trying to remember where I had heard that name.

"Yeh, Middleville, where Billy Motley is pastor. He asked me to come and be his assistant. He was impressed with the bold stand I took at Lime Creek for elder rule. He said he could use a man like me."

"You are going to be Billy Motley's assistant? Billy Motley---the guy who was responsible for the trouble at Lime Creek and in my church as well. What happened to the change of mind you had over the way you handled the situation at Lime Creek?"

I could only shake my head and roll my eyes in unbelief! He continued to act strictly on the basis of impulse and emotion without doctrinal understanding and grounding--- like so many churches as a whole.

20

What Saith the New Testament....?

I tried to encourage Todd to wait and let me approach Lime Creek about giving him another chance, but he wouldn't hear of it. He was too excited (why I do not know) about going to be an assistant to Billy Motley. Understandably this news did not contribute to my ability to sleep that night---something I was having enough trouble doing since the shooting without this to trouble me now.

I was eager the next day (it was Wednesday by now) to tackle the question of the transition between the Old Testament people of God and the New Testament people of God concerning the matter of elders. Was there a continuation of elder leadership, or was there some change going into the era of the New Testament church?

As I looked through my concordance, I noted numerous uses of the word "elder" (presbuteros in the Greek) in the New Testament which made it very clear that the Jews of the New Testament period continued the use of elders as part of their leadership. I noted the following verses and phrases:

Mt 15:2---the disciples transgressed the tradition of the <u>elders</u>

Mt 16:21---Christ must suffer many things from the <u>elders</u>

Mt 21:23---the chief priests and <u>elders</u> came to Christ

Mt 26:3---the chief priests, and the scribes, and the <u>elders</u> of the people assembled to the palace of Caiphas

Mt 26:47---Judas came from the chief priests and the <u>elders</u> of the people

Mt 26:59---the chief priests and <u>elders</u> and all the council sought false witness against Jesus

Mt 27:1---all the chief priests and <u>elders</u> of the people took counsel against Jesus

Mt 27:3---Judas brought the thirty pieces of silver to the priests and <u>elders</u>

Mt 27:20---the chief priests and <u>elders</u> persuaded the multitude to ask for Barabbas and destroy Jesus

Mt 27:41---the chief priests mocked Christ with the scribes and <u>elders</u>

Mt 28:12---the chief priests (vs 11) and the <u>elders</u> took counsel and gave much money to the soldiers

Mk 7:3---the Pharisees and all the Jews were holding the tradition of the <u>elders</u> concerning eating

Mk 7:5---the disciples were not walking according to the tradition of the <u>elders</u>

Mk 8:31---the Son of man must be rejected by the <u>elders</u> and by the chief priests and scribes

Mk 11:27---the chief priests, scribes and <u>elders</u> came to Jesus as He was in the temple

Mk 14:43---Judas came from the chief priests and the scribes and the <u>elders</u>

Mk 14:53---with the high priest was assembled all the chief priests and the <u>elders</u> and the scribes

Mk 15:1---the chief priests held a consultation with the <u>elders</u> and scribes and the whole council

Lk 7:3---a certain centurion's servant sent the <u>elders</u>
of the Jews to Jesus

Lk 9:22---the Son of man must be rejected by the <u>elders</u>
and chief priests and scribes

Lk 20:1---the chief priests and the scribes came unto
Christ in the temple with the <u>elders</u>

Lk 22:52---Jesus spoke to the chief priests and captains
of the temple and <u>elders</u> who came to him

Lk 22:66---the <u>elders</u> of the people, the chief priests and
the scribes came to lead Christ to the council

Acts 4:5---the rulers and <u>elders</u> and scribes (and others)
gathered together at Jerusalem to persecute the
church

Acts 4:8---Peter said to them, Ye rulers of the people,
and <u>elders</u> of Israel

Acts 4:23---after persecution the believers reported all
the chief priests and <u>elders</u> had said unto them

Acts 6:12---certain ones of the synagogue stirred the
people and the <u>elders</u> and the scribes who came
on Stephen and brought him to the council

Looking at these verses, which spoke of the Jews in the
New Testament era, I drew the following conclusions:

1. Elders were part of the Jewish structure of leadership and authority in the New Testament times.

2. Other primary offices of leadership included chief
   priests and scribes.

3. The elders were a leadership group from the lay
   people, the priests were a religious ministry group,
   and the scribes were the experts in the law.

4. Thus the primary leadership group, which was free
    of ministry and law responsibilities, was the group
    known as elders.

5. Thus when the New Testament era fully arrived, the
    office of the priesthood would be obsolete due to
    the work of the great high priest, Christ. The
    scribes, experts on the meticulous keeping of the
    law would fade as well with the message of
    salvation by grace as opposed to the Jewish mis-
    conception of salvation by the Old Testament law.

6. Thus, we should not be surprised if the group
    known as the elders would emerge as a primary
    position of leadership in the church.

7. The question then becomes, did the New Testament
    church continue the office of elder, and if not, was
    there a change in the office and ministry of the elder,
    which moved the people of God from being an elder
    led body to a congregationally ruled people. If that
    was the case, then there should be clear evidence of
    such a change in the New Testament.

8. No discussion of the matter of church government
    in the New Testament can ignore the Old Testament
    background and the context of the Jewish people of
    the New Testament times. One cannot invade the
    New Testament times with a twentieth century
    mentality of democracy to force such a concept on
    a culture far different. If congregational rule is to
    be found in the New Testament, it must be admitted,
    but if that is so, evidence and explanation of the

change must be clearly shown and not just assumed from the basis of arguments and implications not found fully in the Scripture.

9. Our next pursuit must be to determine the matter of leadership positions in the New Testament church, along with any indications of congregational rule.

My thoughts and note-taking were interrupted at this point by a knock on the door. Terry answered it, and Dink came bubbling into the living room where I was sitting in my easy chair. I was glad he had come as I wanted to ask him a question, but he beat me to the punch with a shocking but welcome statement.

"Preacha, I tink I know who gotcha wit da bullet!"

21

Who Give Me Da Bullet....?

It was clear that Dink had come for more than a sick call on his pastor. He had come to share his latest bit of "research" concerning the shooting. I should have known that he would stretch out the suspense in his own unique manner.

"What's his name?" I demanded.

"Whose name?" he countered with a sly grin.

"The shooter's name!" I demanded again.

"You ask da Dink, what's his name?" he said as he seemed to be playing games with me.

"Yes, who is he?" I demanded again.

"Preacha, youse askin da wrong quetsion!" he stated lulling me further into his game.

"Well then, what should my question be?" I spoke with some bewilderment and exasperation.

"You needs to be askin, what's her name?" he shared as he finally got to the point.

"What's her name?" I asked puzzlingly with an emphasis on 'her.'

"Yep, ya needs to ask, what's her name!"

"Ok, what's her name then?" I asked, no longer befuddled, but now impatient.

"Her name is Mandy Collier. Betcha don't know her!" he stated again enjoyingly.

I finally met him head on with a smile.

"Look, Dink, we can play this game all day long. Spill the beans! Tell me every thing you know about her and the shooting situation and how you know these things and anything else."

"Well, she ain't much of a looker---ain't much of a human bein' period! But she's da one tryin to get Troy but got you instead."

"But what about the guy who called me on the phone? That wasn't a girl---unless she has an awfully deep voice," I protested.

"Oh, dat's her boy friend. He's 'bout as low-life as his woithless girl friend. He's pullin da trigger for her."

"But why do they want to shoot Troy?" I asked.

"Well, dat's the sixty-two million shmakeroos question. I don't know why. I jus' know who!"

"But can we prove it?" I queried again. "It won't do any good to know who, if we can't do anything to stop them."

"Nope, I ain't got no proof, and my sources of info ain't got no proof. Give da old Dink some more time, and I might get dat info too, or maybe we could go persuade dem to tell us why."

I didn't quite know what he meant by "persuade," and I didn't ask. But I did reply

"Well, Dink, see what more you can find out, and let me pray about what our next move should be. You have no doubt about the fact that they are behind the shootings?"

When he answered with a solid affirmative, I knew I had to give this some quick attention. Troy's life might depend on it. But what could I do without proof? Did I dare tell Troy without proof? And what if Dink's information was wrong? I was caught in the middle of a dilemma which could turn into a catastrophe no matter what direction I took. Pray about it I would---but we had to do something soon.

That evening, after a good nap, I turned to my study pursuit again. I decided to look at a couple of New Testament passages that spoke of elders, to see if these would be helpful in building some understanding of the government of the church.

Remembering that the Old Testament people of God were led by elders, and that the Jews of the New Testament era were also led by elders, I looked at Acts 11:30 and Acts 14:23, two of the earliest references to elders in the church.

First, I turned to Acts 11:30, which declared that the church at Antioch wanted to send a love gift to the church in Jerusalem.

Which also they did, and sent it to the <u>elders</u> by the hands of Barnabas and Saul."

It wasn't the definitive passage on the subject, but it did declare several things about elders and the church at Jerusalem. I listed several thoughts on the subject:

1. There were elders (presbuteroi) in the church at Jerusalem.

2. There was a plurality of elders in the Jerusalem church.

3. There was some authority or leadership quality in the office of the elders (though this is not spelled out fully) in the Jerusalem church. They were the ones to whom the love gift was sent.

I then turned to Acts 14:23 which stated:

> *And when they had ordained <u>elders</u> in every church, and had prayed with fasting, they commended them to the Lord on whom they believed.*

I had to conclude the following from this verse:

1. Paul traveled on his first missionary journey and ordained/appointed elders in every church.

2. This indicates a plurality of elders in each church.

Though my study was so far very limited, I could at this point state from these two verses:

1. Elders were leaders in the New Testament churches.
2. Elders were in a plurality in the New Testament churches.
3. Elders were appointed by an apostle here (Paul).

22

Elders and More Elders....!

I went to bed that Wednesday night after my conversation with Dink, but I couldn't sleep. A question was burning in my brain. What would be the best approach to Miss Mandy Collier concerning her involvement in the shooting incident?

I decided I needed to know more about her---who she was, where she lived, etc.---before I could plot a strategy. I had also decided not to tell Troy, because I had no proof, and because he was so personally involved. But there was a problem---it would be several more days before I would be mobile. How could I contact any one about these matters?

I decided to call Dink and ask him to get all the information he could about Mandy Collier and her boy friend. That would help me form some plan to contact her. I warned him to gather the information anonymously, but he didn't seem to know what I meant till I explained, and then he laughed that I, of all people, would try to tell him how to do his work. So I left it in his hands with much prayer!

This left the remainder of the day for me to pursue the elder matter. I moved to the verse mentioning elders in Acts 15.

2 When, therefore, Paul and Barnabas had no small dissension and disputation with them [certain men

*who had come to them from Judea], they determined
Paul and Barnabas, and certain other of them, should
go up to Jerusalem unto the apostles and <u>elders</u> about
this question.*

*4   And when they were come to Jerusalem, they were
received by the church and the apostles and <u>elders</u>,
and they declared all things that God had done with
them.*

*6   And the apostles and <u>elders</u> came together to
consider this matter.*

These were the verses prior to the meeting of the
Jerusalem council. I also noted several matters:

1. Paul and Barnabas were sent to Jerusalem to the
   apostles and <u>elders</u> concerning this major doctrinal
   matter (the Jewish-Gentile problem).

2. Paul and Barnaabas upon arriving at Jerusalem were
   received by the apostles and <u>elders</u>.

3. Paul and Barnabas declared all their experience in
   this doctrinal matter to apostles and <u>elders</u>.

4. The apostles and <u>elders</u> came together to consider
   this important doctrinal issue.

Next I looked at the verses following the meeting of the
council in Jerusalem in the latter part of Acts 15.

*22   Then it pleased the apostles and <u>elders</u> with the
whole church, to send chosen men of their own
company to Antioch with Paul and Barnabas, namely,*

Judas, surnamed Barsabbas, and Silas, chief men among the brethren.
23 And they wrote letters by them after this manner: The apostles and <u>elders</u> and brethren send greeting unto the brethren who are of the Gentiles in Antioch and Syria and Cilicia.

I noted again several ideas from the passage:

1. The apostles and <u>elders</u> continue to be the ones mentioned as leaders of the church following the council meeting in Jerusalem.

2. The apostles and <u>elders</u> sent men from Jerusalem to Antioch to help spread the decision of the council.

3. The apostles and <u>elders</u> sent a message to the brethren who are of the Gentiles in Antioch and Syria and Cilicia.

Thus, I had to conclude from these verses, both prior to and following the Jerusalem council, that the apostles and elders were the leaders of the churches of the New Testament era. They dealt authoritatively with this most important doctrinal problem.

I couldn't help but wonder where the deacons were in this passage. It was obvious they were not involved in authoritative leadership. Could they still have been occupied with the duties they performed when the office was first mentioned in Acts 6?

I needed to take note to check this out further as the study progressed.

A few hours after finishing my meditation on this passage, I got a phone call from Todd. He just wanted to touch base with me. He had moved to his new field, and was rejoicing. To hear him tell it, there was no place on earth like Middleville Baptist Church. And there was no one like Billy Motley. It was heaven on earth---maybe even the millennium---maybe even heaven itself. No more church business meetings. No more complaining people. No more rebellion against authority. And no more uncertainty about who was leading the church.

Todd was so excited, he was convinced he could stay there forever. I smiled and told him I was glad things were going well. I didn't have the heart to tell him I had heard that before---not just from him, but from many others. I did not mean to be a pessimist, but I wondered how long it would last!

23

What of the Overseers....?

The next morning I got another visit from Dink. It seems he had been very busy getting the information I had requested.

"Man, that didn't take you long," I observed.

"Preacha, when ya asks da Dink, ya asks da right man!"

"Well, what can you tell me about Mandy Collier and her boy friend?" I inquired.

"Ya won't believe it, Preacha, but her boy friend is a former preacha too!" Dink said with some pride over his gathering of the facts. "He used ta pastoh out west some where. His name is Phil, uh, Phil Millow. Widout quetsion, he's da one tottin da pistol for Mandy. Its her problem, but he's da gun totter He's got some job at Bully Boy Mills doin somethin or other. He ain't got no jail record. Nobody seems ta understand what he's doin wit Mandy or what he could see in her. If he was a preacha, he's sure turned sour!"

"Now what about Mandy?" I asked again.

"Well, Preacha, if I ain't saved, I could tell you better bout her! But since gettin saved and gettin rid of some of my vocab, I can't be as pacific. She's da scum of da earth, an when I say scum, I mean scum! Der ain't nuttin she ain't into. She's mean as that old snake, da devil. Preacha, you don't want ta mess wit her."

"Okay, but did you run into any idea of a motive. Why are they after Troy?"

Dink had no idea of a motive.

After inquiring further about where they lived, which Dink knew also, I had another question.

"Dink, how can I meet them or even talk to one of them about the Lord without their knowing I know they are the ones after Troy? Maybe Phil would be the weak link, since he seemed to have a conscience and called me when he missed Troy and got me instead."

"Preacha, give me a day or so and I'll have a plan---a poifect plan---a Dink plan!" he promised confidently.

With that, he left, and so I turned again to my pursuit of the matter of elders. I had been looking at the subject of elders in the book of Acts. Thus far I had seen that elders, along with the apostles, were the leaders of the early church. Now I wanted to look at the next several references to elders in Acts. The first verse I considered was Acts 20:17, which read:

And from Miletus he sent to Ephesus, and called the *elders* *of the church.*

Paul was on his third missionary journey. So when passing through Miletus, he called the elders of the church in Ephesus to give them some final counsel. He knew he was going soon to Jerusalem, but did not know if he would see them beyond that hour. The seriousness of the hour is evidenced in verse 37. When he had finished his counsel, and after praying with them, they wept much and fell on his neck and kissed him.

As I read this verse, several thoughts ran through my mind:

1. Paul called the elders on this important occasion, indicating again they were the leaders of the church.

2. Paul did not call the deacons. I wrote in the margin of my Bible, "Why didn't Paul call the deacons, if they were the spiritual leaders of the church?" This was another indication, as I had noted before, that the deacons were not the spiritual leaders of the church.

3. Paul called the elders (plural) of the church. This seems to indicate again a plurality of elders in the church, for the word church in verse 17 is singular and not plural.

The next verse I noted was Acts 20:28. Though Paul does not use the word elder (presbuteros), he does use an interesting word related to elder, the word episkopos, as a reference to the same group noted as elders in verse 17. As Paul charges them, he says:

Take heed, therefore, unto yourselves, and to all the flock, over which the Holy Spirit hath made you overseers (episkopous, the plural of episkopos), to feed the church of God which he hath purchased with his own blood.

I noted again several ideas from this passage.

1. The terms presbuteros and episkopos refer to the
    same office as Paul uses them interchangeably
    in verses 17 and 28. Thus, the elder is a bishop
    and the bishop is an elder.

2. The difference in the words is a matter, it seems, of
    the various duties of the office. Episkopos stresses
    ministry (take heed to the flock and feed the flock),
    while presbuteros refers to the ruling and leadership
    aspect of the elder. But the point is that these words
    speak of the same office, though they speak of the
    different responsibilities of the office.

I asked myself another question, as I was closing my
thinking on these verses. Why did not Dr. Frakes, as he
argued for congregational rule, deal with some of these
passages, if for no other reason than to answer the
arguments of those advocating elder rule?

I was eager now to begin studying this subject with the
deacons, as they had agreed. This life in the house was
getting to me.

24

Rulers in the Church....?

I had barely gotten up the next morning, and was hardly ready to receive visitors, when who should show up at the front door but good old Dink. He was taking his assignment almost as a divine mandate. But I had to admit, he was always a joy to be around---something of a naiveté in the faith with some simplistic wisdom and insight.

"Hey, Preacha! How ya doin?" he asked with a consuming smile.

"Well, pretty well," I answered. "But don't look for me in the pulpit tomorrow. What's new with you?"

"Preacha, I gots da plan! You asked me to get a plan, and, Preacha, I gots da plan!"

I was eager to hear his plan, but knew I had to assess it carefully lest it be somewhat off the wall in light of Dink's enthusiasm but immaturity in the Lord.

"Here's what we goin ta do, Preacha. One of da boys knows him, this Phil Millow guy, da shooter, and Phil knows we been saved. And we been witnessin to ever body. It would be spected dat we witness to him. But we ain't yet. He probly wonders why we ain't talked to him yet. And, Preacha, we could take you wid us."

I must admit, I was impressed with the plan. Even if Phil suspected something, we wouldn't say a word about that, but only talk to him of Christ. And we would let the Lord take it from there.

I agreed to his plan, but the only problem was that I wouldn't be able to go with them for several more days. So I suggested that he, and whoever it was who knew Phil, visit him in the home to witness to him about his relationship with the Lord and nothing else. Let that set the stage for a future visit when I could go along with them. Dink agreed, and said he would do it as soon as possible, and let me know. Then he was gone.

After some breakfast and my devotions, I turned to my pursuit of the subject which had come to possess my thinking. My next verse of concern (as I was moving through the New Testament) was in Romans, and contained a reference to ruling. It was Romans 12:8 and stated that the one ruling was to rule with diligence.

In looking at the setting of the passage, I noted the following:

1. This phrase is in the early portion of the practical section of Romans, that is, the early part of 12-16.

2. The section begins with a challenge to commitment (verses 1-2).

3. The phrase then is found in the next section, which speaks of the church as the body and the differing gifts the Lord has given to the body, and how they are to be administered:

   a. prophecy according to the proportion of faith 6
   b. ministry in the spirit of a minister 7
   c. teaching in the spirit of a teacher 7
   d. exhortation in the spirit of exhortation 8

    e.   giving in the spirit of liberality 8

    f.   <u>ruling</u> in the spirit of diligence 8

In looking at the Greek word, I discovered it was a nominative, singular, masculine, present middle participle from proistemi, and it carried the meaning of presiding, governing, or superintending. In the middle mood it could also mean to practice diligently or to maintain the practice of something. I noted it was used in several other places in the New Testament, namely I Thessalonians 5:12; I Timothy 3:4-5 and 12; I Timothy 5:17 and Titus 3:8 and 14. I noted these passages read as follows:

I Thessalonians 5:12

> *We beseech you, brethren, to know them who labor among you, and are <u>over you</u> (accusative plural masculine, present middle participle) in the Lord, and admonish you.*

I Timothy 3:4-5

> *...one that <u>ruleth</u> (aorist infinitive) well his own house, having his children in subjection with all gravity. For if a man knows not how to <u>rule</u> (not proistemi but epimelomai) his own house, how shall he take care of the church of God?*

I Timothy 3:12

> *Let the deacons be the husbands of one wife, <u>ruling</u> (nominative, plural, masculine, present middle participle) their children and their own houses well.*

I Timothy 5:17

> *Let the elders that rule (nominative, plural masculine, present participle) well, be counted worthy of double honor, especially those who labor in word and doctrine.*

Titus 3:8

> *This is a faithful saying, and these things I will that thou affirm constantly, that they who have believed in God might be careful <u>to maintain</u> (present infinitive middle) good works.*

Titus 3:14

> *And let ours also learn <u>to maintain</u> (present infinitive middle) good works for necessary uses, that they be not unfruitful.*

Concerning these verses I noted the following:

1. The Greek word proistemi has two different meanings and both meanings are mirrored in the verses above.

2. The two meanings are, first, to rule over or preside over, and secondly, to maintain.

3. The usage of ruling or presiding is used as follows:

    a. in a general manner simply referring to those who rule over the church as in the Romans 12:8 and I Thessalonians 5:12 passages with no reference as to who these rulers are (elders, etc.)

      b. in a particular manner indicating those ruling over the church are the elders as in I Timothy 3:4-5 and I Timothy 5:17.

4. There is the usage of maintaining as in Titus 3:8 and 14, but this use has no reference to the elders, only to believers in general.

5. There is no use of the word (ruling) in reference to deacons ruling in the church. The only reference to deacons is in relation to their responsibility to rule their families.

I also took note that this agreed with what I had found in Acts---that the elders were the leaders in the church, and not the deacons. I also noted that in light of the Acts passages, and these other passages, which also refer to elders as the ones ruling, I could conclude that the general passages, which refer to ruling (Romans 12:8 and I Thessalonians 5:12) probably are speaking of the elders also.

25

What of the Office of Pastor....?

The next day was Sunday, and though I was not able to preach, I did go to the morning service. It was good to see the people. They had kept in touch these two weeks by telephone, since the shooting, but now it was good to see them in person.

Even Dink was full of exuberance---more so than usual. He couldn't wait till the service was over to tell me of his witnessing to Phil Millow, so he tried to accost me even during the prelude.

He began to speak in a whisper, but I had to assure him that as eager as I was to hear his news, we had better wait till the service was over. That made it difficult for me to concentrate on the sermon preached by Todd. I has asked him to preach for me, but I had also given him clear and definite instructions to stay off the subject of church government.

When church was over, Todd also asked if I had time to talk with him. He shared with me that some early impressions at Middleville Baptist Church really bothered him. We made an appointment for him to stop by and see me on Monday so we could talk about the matter in full without interruption or rush.

That left me free to talk to Dink. I invited him over for lunch, knowing Terry wouldn't care. He was elated at the invitation, and eager to speak the moment he walked in my front door. But Terry made us promise not to say anything till she could listen also. So when we sat down at the table, after we had prayed, Dink began his story.

"Preacha, we talked to ol Phil las night! We went ta his house and he was all by himself---on Saturday night, too. We jus tod him bout Jesus! We said nuttin bout nuttin else. When we was done, he tanked us, and said he had wondered when we was gonna talk ta him, cause he knew we'd been saved---me and so many of da boys. We invited him to chuch, and he said he jus might come, but den we'se heard dat from lots of folks. But maybe he'll come!"

"Did my name come up in the conversation?" I asked.

"Yeh, we always tell folks about our pastoh. We tod him youse da best!"

"Did he say anything about how he used to be a preacher?" I quizzed further.

"Yeh, in fact he did. He said he had left da ministry cause of old Mandy. It was ten years ago---when they was a good bit younger. He left his wife, family and chuch for that ol gal. Whadda bum decision dat was!"

"Is there anything else I need to know about the visit?" I queried.

"Yeh, der was one ting more. He hadda few tears in his eyes afta we prayed for him. Can ya imagine dat. Old hard-hearted, backslidden, Mandy-lovin Phil was cryin!"

Dink was not speaking sacrastically or in jest. Rather, he was very serious for once in his life, expressing in his words a real concern.

"Preacha, he had no idee we was knowin he was da shooter! Da door's open for us to go back an fur you ta go wid us. Let me know when, Preacha."

This certainly was good news, and I looked forward to going with Dink and the boys to see him---as soon as possible.

I didn't do much the rest of the day, seeing it was the Lord's day. But Monday morning, bright and early, I was at my pursuit once again. I thought it might be good to summarize what I had discovered and concluded so far in my study. I noted the following thoughts:

1. Elder leadership was prevalent in the Old Testament era.

2. Elder leadership was prevalent also in the New Testament period among the Jews.

3. Elder leadership clearly was present also in the New Testament church according to the book of Acts.

4. The terms "elder" and "bishop" were interchangeable words for the same New Testament office, stressing different aspects of the same office.

5. Thus far the office of deacon had not surfaced as an office of leadership in the New Testament church.

The passage I wanted to look at next was Ephesians 4:11 and its context. The verse reads as follows:

And he gave some, apostles; and some, prophets; and some, evangelists; and some, pastors and teachers.

This verse and its context speaks of some of the offices of the New Testament church. I recorded these thoughts about what I knew of these offices:

1. The apostles were the God-called men who were involved in the establishment of the New Testament church. They were the recipients of divine revelation, and in many cases, the writers of the New Testament. This office ceased with the completion of the New Testament.

2. The office of prophet was the other foundational office of the New Testament church, according to Ephesians 2:20.

3. The office of evangelist was, it seems, a continuing one with the duties of the proclamation of the gospel message.

4. The questions surround the next two words, pastors and teachers, with the greatest discussion being whether this speaks of one office or two. Was there a single office of a pastor-teacher, or were there two offices, one of pastor and another of a teacher.

As I looked at my Greek New Testament, and made some exegetical notations, I came to the conclusion that this was just one office for the following reason:

Because of the Granville-Sharp rule, which states that "When the copulative kai connects two nouns of the same case, if the article ho or any of its cases precedes the first of the said nouns or participles, and is not repeated before the second noun or participle, the latter always relates to the same person that is expressed or described by the first noun or participle; that is, it denotes a further description of the first-named person."

I realized as one reads that rule, or as I would share it with my deacons or church, it surely would need some explanation.   I wrote on my notes the following explanations:

The above speaks of two possible constructions in the Greek:

1. <u>Possibility One</u>

the Greek---tous poimenas kai didaskalous
the English---the shepherds and teachers

This construction would speak of just one office since the article "tous" or "the" is not repeated before the second noun, but is used only once and that is before the first noun. This means that the article governs both nouns, causing us to conclude that only one person is being indicated.

2. <u>Possibility Two</u>

the Greek---tous poimenas kai tous didaskalous
the English---the shepherds and the teachers

This construction would speak of two persons
or offices since the article "tous" or "the" is
repeated before the second noun, rather than
being found just before the first noun. This
means each article governs the noun with
which it is used, thus indicating two persons
or offices.

The construction in our verse, Ephesians 4:11, is that of possibility number one. Thus, the conclusion was that we have another office, that of pastor/teacher, in the New Testament church besides the elders or bishops. That is we do not have two more offices, that of a pastor and another one titled teacher. No, it is pastor/teacher --- a single office.

The question I now had to face was if this office of pastor/teacher was the same as the elder/bishop office as some claimed.

That study would have to wait for another time, for the hour of my appointment with Todd was growing near. I was anxious to hear of what was disturbing him at Middleville Baptist Church.

26

Trouble in an Elder-led Church....?

When I had finished the notes on the pastor/teacher, I stretched out in my comfortable living room chair to rest for a few minutes. I marveled that I was feeling better, and even stronger, but it was a little difficult getting the old energy back

I could have gone back to sleep, but then the doorbell rang. Knowing it had to be Todd, I called for him to come in, which he did.

I greeted him with a cheerful hello, but didn't get much cheer back---not even a hello.

"Ira, I wish I had never heard the term elder!" he blurted out. "I'd be happy if I'd never hear it again!"

I had detected on Sunday that he was not happy with some things at Middleville, but I had no idea things were so critical. I urged him to tell me about it.

"Well, it appears to me that the elders over there want to control my life---every aspect of it!" he confessed with deep concern.

As he rattled on, I got the picture of a group of church leaders out of control. They had already informed him that he had to live with one of the single elders and learn servanthood by cleaning his house, washing his clothes, and doing anything else he instructed him to do. The idea was that Todd had to learn submission to authority---the authority of the elders.

Furthermore, they had instructed him he was no longer to go to school for they would teach him. Even more serious was their statement they would constantly assess his call to the ministry, and if they concluded he was not called, they would instruct him, and he would be assigned another ministry in the church, which he would be expected to fulfill without question.

And to top it off, if he ever wanted to get married, they would be the ones to guide him in the choice of a mate, and even have final approval or rejection of the girl he would chose to marry. They already had a girl in mind, but would not at this point indicate who she was. They indicated that would come out in time after he had proven himself.

He continued with his woeful analysis.

"Ira, you wouldn't believe it over there. They have a dozen or more young men who were called to preach, and some have even had invitations to pastor, but the elders will not let them leave the church to pastor or work in another church. It's a dictatorship!"

By now he was almost screaming in disgust.

"And that's not all!" he hurried to inform me. "They discipline people for being overweight, underweight, and other reasons I'm not sure are Biblical! Ira, what am I going to do?"

My reply was easy.

"Well, if you've got any sense at all you'll stay as far away from that place as you can. This is a church which has allowed elder-leadership to drift into legalism and authoritarianism with the elders seeking to play Holy Spirit in every one's life, setting as normative and absolute matters which Scripture does not. If you stay there you will soon be in so deep you can't get out."

"But where will I go?" he asked pitifully. "I have burned my bridges at Lime Creek, and now I have nowhere to go. And will Middleville Baptist let me out of the commitment I have already made to them?"

"You've made a commitment to them already?" I asked in astonishment.

Now I got firm.

"Todd, get out and get out now! Then worry about what the Lord wants you to do next!"

He left almost in tears, and to be honest, I wasn't sure what he would do.

I sat and let my mind rest for a few moments as I plopped back in my lounge chair. Several thoughts came to my mind, which I had to note for future reference:

1. Elder rule, if Scriptural, could deteriorate into legalism and authoritarianism unless there is the following:

    a. a clear understanding of the role and duty of the elders

    b. a clear understanding of the need of a balance of the elders' leadership authority and the work of the Holy Spirit in the members' lives---such a balance so delicate that it would be easy for the elders to become legalistic, as it would for the members to become sinfully independent of the established leadership of the church

    c. a clear understanding of the necessity of a method of accountability for the elders where-

by extremes could be recognized, challenged
and dealt with

d. a sensitivity among the elders to reject any
legalistic and authoritarian spirit and to embrace a spirit of humility, grace, and love in
the leading of the church

e. a submissiveness in the heart of the member,
but not a blind submission which would in
any manner enslave the member's life and
conscience to the authority of man rather than
the authority of God

I was beginning to understand how delicate and difficult
a matter this thing called "church government" was.
Congregational rule could easily become anarchy of the
multitudes, while elder leadership could easily become a
dictatorship by a few.

27

Why Are You Trying to Kill Troy....?

I felt so good at the end of Monday, that I determined Tuesday evening would be the time to go see Phil Millow with Dink. If that went well, I would plan to be in the pulpit the following Sunday. I was getting anxious now to get back into the usual schedule, but knew I had better use some wisdom in this decision. Thus, I rested all day Tuesday, not even working on the elder matter.

After supper, Dink picked me up. I might have been better off to drive myself than to ride in Dink's vehicle--- something that looked like a World War II Jeep. I wondered how good it was for me to bounce around as we did going to Phil Millow's house.

When we pulled up in front of a house and stopped, I was shocked. It was a run-down, beat-up place, which was badly in need of repair and paint. The steps of the porch and the porch itself creaked as we walked over it. I wondered if it would hold our weight.

From the porch I could hear loud music with resonant bass sounds rattling the windows. Though I was not trying to look in the window, it was impossible not to see inside as the shades were open. Someone was there.

Dink knocked loudly on the rough paintless door. And he yelled out with boldness, "Anybody home? Its da Dink and Pastoh Ira!" Nothing like broadcasting our entrance, I thought to myself.

As the door creaked open, I saw a man through the screen who was peering into the night, trying to see who it was. Dink's message identifying us had been drowned out by the music.

"Its Dink and Pastoh Ira!" he bellowed even louder this time, as he opened the screen door.

As the door opened and we walked in, I was shocked at the evident testimony standing before me of the results of sin in a man's life. Phil looked years older than his age. His voice was soft, and I did recognize it as the one on the phone. I thought he had been disguising his voice on the phone by speaking softly, but that was his real voice. He sounded and looked tired, but he welcomed us with a grimace of pain.

Dink introduced me, and as we shook hands, I also sensed a weakness in his grip. He offered us a seat on the sofa, which also was old and dilapidated with the springs popping out in places. A stale smell of smoke permeated the room.

Dink, in his usual manner, directly and boldly began the conversation.

"Mistuh Phil, you ready to get right with God tonight?"

His method was not to be found in any of the evangelism books I had read, but the writers of the books had never met Dink! The boldness didn't seem to bother Phil---I guess he knew Dink.

Phil broke down and began to cry with obvious and consuming sobs---so much that he couldn't speak. He could only bury his head in his hands.

And then he spoke through the tears and sobs.

"I wish I would have died ten years ago! How can I ever live down what I have been, done and become over that time when I turned my back on my Lord, trampled His law, cursed and even blasphemed His name, and contradicted in my life all I know to be holy! I would be better off dead even today, for it appears I am paying for my rebellion and desertion from Him and His call on my life. I am a modern Jonah, who has been sinking in the sea of not just godless living, but perverted reprobate living. What a fool! What a fool! What a fool!" he kept repeating as he sobbed.

At this point Dink seemed willing to let me speak to him. So I dealt with him extensively concerning the reality of his salvation. Had he really been saved? Or was he like so many who had made a profession, but had never experienced regeneration?

After this spiritual grilling, he still maintained he had no doubt about his salvation. God had arrested him as a young man, saved him, called him to preach, and had used him in powerful ministry for more than a decade until he had met Mandy Collier. She had joined the church he pastored, and was the epitome of beauty and charm in those days. He yielded to her seductive ways and left his wife and family and church for all she appeared to promise. But then in a few months he was sorry for what he had done! By then it was too late to change his decision She had led him into not only illicit actions, but had implicated him in illegal activities, for which she could frame him and send him to jail if he didn't go along with her. She had used these crimes to keep him in line---always threatening to go to the police if he ever left her! He was too weak and broken to fight her strong dominating will.

I had never heard a sadder story, or seen a more broken man, nor heard a more convincing testimony of the foolishness of sin. My heart went out to him, and I struggled concerning what I could say. I now understood why he was willing to be her pawn in trying to kill Troy, though I did not know her motive for the action.

And then he blurted it out, evidently so convicted he could not keep it in.

"And now I have stooped so low that I have been trying to kill a man. And Brother Pointer, I almost killed you instead. How could God ever forgive me?"

In an instant I knew I had to go in one of several directions in the conversation. I either had to assure him that God could forgive him, or bluntly ask him why he had been trying to kill Troy, or both.

I began with the one concerning his sin to see if his repentance was real.

"Why are you trying to kill Troy?" I blurted out. "You say you want God's forgiveness, then you must begin with a clean sweep of this matter of trying to kill Troy. Why are you trying to kill Troy?"

When he didn't answer, I repeated the question with great insistence.

"WHY ARE YOU TRYING TO KILL TROY MEDFORD?"

28

What Is the Work of a Pastor....?

I was waiting expectantly for Phil to answer my question about why he had been trying to kill Troy, when the enemy did his work. So many times, it seems, when in a witnessing situation, Satan interrupts. And in this situation, he surely did interrupt as Mandy herself came through the front door!

She quickly assessed the situation, and seeing the broken condition of Phil, she blew her top. She lit into him with a vulgar tongue-lashing such as I had never heard. She began throwing things around the room, and ordered us out of the house.

I was hoping Phil would stand up to her, but that proved to be too much to ask. He quickly exited the room, leaving us with her wrath, and she vented herself again with a worse barrage of language than before. She finally ordered us out of the house with the command never to come back.

At this point I figured I couldn't make her any madder, and that she would not do any thing more than she had done, so I decided to leave a strong witness with her.

"Mandy, this is the first time we have met, and I don't know why you are so upset with our being here. We have only come for one purpose---to tell you and Phil of God's grace and mercy to sinners. The Bible says the wages of sin is death, but the gift of God is eternal life!"

At this point she interrupted me. I was surprised I had gotten that far. She informed me she knew all about preachers, and that if she was younger, she would do to me what she had done to Phil---ruin my life! Then she walked out of the room.

I looked at Dink, and he was ready to go after her, but I grabbed him and stopped him. It was obvious we could do nothing now but leave and put the matter in God's hands. I was disappointed that we had been so close to helping Phil, and finding out the reason for Mandy wanting to kill Troy, yet so far, we were still in the dark

I asked Dink to pray as we sat outside in the car. I rejoiced to hear him pray and acknowledge all these matters were in the hands of our "sovern" God, and that God would have His way in the matter regardless of a rebellious sinner.

I hardly slept that night---too much emotional and spiritual upheaval and too much burden to pray. I got up a little later than normal the next morning, and after the usual morning responsibilities, I returned to my study pursuit.

Having established the office of pastor/teacher in the last study, I decided to continue my study of Ephesians 4:11-16. As I dug out the context I discovered the following truths.

I   WHAT GOD HAS DONE   4:11

God gave the leaders of 4:11 to the church
    apostles
    prophets
    evangelists
    pastor/teachers

II WHY GOD DID THIS 4:12

so these leaders could
   thoroughly prepare
   or thoroughly equip the saints

so these saints when equipped could
   do the works of righteousness
   and build the body of Christ

III WHAT GOAL DID GOD HAVE 4:13-16

until all the saints would arrive
   at the unity of faith
   at the unity of the knowledge of God
   at the full development as men of God
   at the full development of the stature of Christ

with the end
   they would no longer be babes in Christ
     who are being tossed to and fro
     who are being born about
       by every wind of doctrine
       by the deception of men
       by the cunning wiles of seduction
   they speak the truth in love
   they may grow up in Christ their Head
    in all things
    to the advancement of the body in love
    as His body being correctly joined together
       by every joint of supply
       according to the active power
        of every part

To put it all in a nutshell, God gave these gifted leaders to the church so they could prepare and qualify the church for ministry, so that these saints in the church could do the work of the ministry, and so they would no longer be babes in Christ, but would reach the full stature of Christ Himself. Then they would be mature doctrinally so they would be fully established and not be blown about by every false idea. They also would be in unity and have His power to do the work of God.

I realized this was not a thorough exposition of the passage, but it did show what purpose and goal God had in giving these leaders to the church.

I noted particularly that the pastor did not have the responsibility of doing all the work of the ministry. His duty was to prepare the saints so they could do the work of the ministry together. The leaders had the primary responsibility of preparing the people for the task.

I noted several other things. Deacons were not in this list of those leaders who equip the church for ministry. I had already noted they were not in the list with the elders as leaders who carried authority in the church. Second, I noted the elders also were not mentioned in this list of leaders who were to equip the church. Could that be because they carried the leadership, but were not teachers and equippers?

I remembered that some had argued for the pastor/teacher being an elder. I made a note to check into this further in my study.

I spent the remainder of the day in thought and prayer for Phil and Mandy. My thoughts and prayer were interrupted by an unexpected phone call!

29

How Did I Get into This....?

On the other end of the line was the soft voice of Phil Millow, and he spoke apologetically.

"Pastor Pointer, I am sorry for the way things went last night! I didn't expect Mandy to come home when she did. I had to leave or it would have been worse. Believe me when I say it would have been worse---much worse!"

Silence followed this initial offering, so I decided to try to steer the conversation.

"Phil, have you given further thought to what we discussed last night? Are you ready to come back to the Lord in repentance and surrender of your life anew to Christ?"

"Preacher meet me tomorrow night and I will tell you the whole story---I don't think I can do it on the phone. Meet me at the Public Park next to the swimming pool. Just park your car in the parking lot at 10:00 P.M. and I will find you. Come alone and I will be alone also."

Then he was gone! The line was dead. As a result I didn't sleep any better that night than I had the previous evening.

The next day was a Thursday. My mind continued to be occupied with the scheduled meeting that night. But I did continue my study. After having looked at elders in the Old Testament period, I had started through the New Testament itself taking note of the words used for the leadership positions in the New Testament church. I had not pursued just one word, but several words concerning leadership, dealing with them as they occurred chronologically in the text.

I had noted the following so far:

1. Elder leadership prevailed in the Old Testament era.

2. Elder leadership clearly was present also in the New Testament period among the Jews.

3. Elder leadership clearly was present also in the New Testament church according to the book of Acts.

4. The terms "elder" and "bishop" were used interchangeably in some places in the New Testament.

5. Thus far the office of deacon had not surfaced as an office of leadership in the New Testament church.

6. There was another office in the New Testament church, that of pastor/teacher, whose work was to equip the saints for the work of the ministry.

7. I still had several unsettled questions:
    a. How did the office of pastor/teacher relate to the office of elder?

    b. What were the duties of the deacons if they were not leaders who carried authority in the New Testament Church?

My next verse was Philippians 1:1, which read:

Paul and Timothy, the servants of Jesus Christ, to all the saints in Christ Jesus who are at Philippi, with the bishops and deacons...

I noted the greeting of Paul was directed in a three-fold manner---to all the saints at Philippi, to the bishops (episkopos), and to the deacons.

Questions began to swirl through my mind: (1) Was the office of pastor/teacher left out because this office was included in the office of elder/bishop? (2) Why was the office of deacon included in this setting and not with the office of elder/bishop in other passages? (3) Could any conclusions be drawn from this brief greeting in Philippians 1:1?

Concerning question number one, I concluded that I would continue to keep my eyes open as I made my journey through the New Testament to see if I would find an answer.

Concerning question number two, I concluded nothing could be made of the office of deacon being listed with the bishops, in light of the fact this was only a greeting and the entire church was also addressed in the term "saints." It did indicate the office of deacon was an active office in the church, but it said nothing of its duties or whether it was an office of authority or service.

Concerning question number three, I concluded I had answered this question in answering the first two.

After resting through out the late afternoon and into the evening, I left home about 9:00 and headed for the park to meet Phil Millow. He had said to come alone, which I was going to do. But I had to confess I had some serious concerns and apprehensions. I began to consider all the possibilities. Was I being set up for some harm? What if Mandy had whipped Phil into line, and now they were going to get rid of one who was getting to know too much about their crime?

I concluded that it was much easier to study the Bible than to face life in its reality. I wondered how I ever got into this! I was comforted to know that it was by His will, and He would control the outcome.

30

What Are You Doing Here....?

I had left home quite early so I could case the place. It took me about ten minutes to get to the park, and then, though it was dark, I drove several blocks around the outer perimeter to see if there were any cars in sight. I saw no cars in the park, so I drove into one of the entrances. I drove up and down the winding streets to see if I could spot anything unusual.

There was not a soul or a car that I could see in the park. I drove back around and stopped in the parking lot of the swimming pool. I backed my car up to one of the buildings so I could see ahead and on the sides, and hoped also no one could slip up from behind. It was still early, but I tried to stay alert to any situation. I kept the key in the ignition and the doors locked in case I needed to make a quick get-away.

I waited and waited. Ten o'clock came and then ten-thirty. I wondered how long I should wait. I wondered what had happened to Phil. Then a car entered the park entrance at some distance---I could see the lights! My heart sped up somewhat, and I took a deep breath. I said to myself, "This is it!"

I watched as the car came slowly down the winding streets. I blew out a breath of air for some relief as the car turned into the swimming pool parking lot. He had on the brightest of bright lights. Then a spotlight hit my windshield blinding me. I put my hands over my face to shut out the light so I could see, but that didn't seem to help. I was more than frightened---I was mortified, petrified and horrified.

I watched as someone got out. He left his lights on the car in my face, and left his spotlight trained on me also. And now he pointed a giant flashlight at me as he walked a few steps toward me. I spied what looked like a gun in his other hand, and my heart began to do back-flips, half-gainers, full-gainers and every dive that this swimming pool had ever seen in all its days.

Then a voice barked at me, "Get out slowly with your hands-up, so I can see them at all times! Don't make one quick move in the process!"

Then he asked a question.

"Brother Ira, is that you?"

I realized it was not Phil Millow, or some hit man sent by Mandy, but it was Troy Medford, my policeman friend. What was he doing here? Not that I wasn't glad to see him! He would have been my first choice at this moment of my life.

"Yes, yes! Its me," I shouted as I rolled down my window.

Troy put down the flashlight, holstered his gun and walked to my car.

He smiled as he asked a rhetorical question

"I didn't scare you, did I?"

But now that I was over my fright, I wanted to know if he had come here as part of his nightly duty, or did someone send him?

"Well, we had a strange call at headquarters. We were told to go to the swimming pool and we would find a dead body? Brother Ira, what are you doing here?"

My mind began to scramble through the few facts I had at this moment. Was I supposed to be that dead body? Was there a dead body near by us right now? What had happened to Phil? Or could it be that someone was drawing Troy to this deserted area to kill him, and maybe even me? And if that was the case, we both had walked right into their trap! And Troy was now standing in the light as a perfect target for someone to shoot him---even from several yards away.

Now I gave the orders to Troy, and I am sure he was shocked.

"Troy, hit the ground and get out of that light---right now---immediately---don't ask any questions. Somebody has set us up!?"

Perhaps his police training and experience convinced him that this was the right thing to do, because he hit the ground like a man without a parachute dropped from an airplane. He scrambled quickly back toward his car to get behind the bright lights. And it didn't take him long to get to the driver's side of his police car, open the door and kill the lights.

Next he started his engine and pulled up in the dark next to me. I was facing out and he was facing in, so my driver's side of the car was next to the driver's side of his.

He now whispered in a strong but hushed voice, "Brother Ira, what is going on here!!??"

"I'm not sure, Troy! But we may be sitting ducks here. Follow me to Handy Andy's and I will try to explain it all to you."

So slumped in our seats, and looking through the steering wheel, barely seeing over the dashboard so we would not be an easy target, we drove out of the park.

As I drove the several blocks to Handy Andy's, I wondered what I was going to tell Troy. Should I tell him the whole story, including who was trying to kill him?

By now it was about eleven o'clock, and I began to feel exhausted---drained physically and emotionally. My mind seemed like a computer chip which whirled and whirled, but never was able to bring up the right program or file.

I could not find the answer to what had gone on tonight! I wondered how close I had come to being the body! I wished I had stayed home and studied about elders, deacons and pastor/teachers.

I pulled into Handy Andy's, but that is all I remembered till I woke up as they were carrying me into the emergency room at the hospital.

31

Do Elders Rule over Us....?

After a number of tests, the hospital concluded that there was nothing really wrong with me except exhaustion. They told me to go home and go to bed and to stay in bed all the next day.

Terry was there, understandably, with a very concerned look on her face, and Troy had stayed to find out how I was. I rode home with Terry and Troy in his squad car. My car was still at Handy Andy's.

As we rode home, Troy finally broke the silence.

"Pastor, I know you don't feel like talking now, and it really wouldn't be the best for you, but could I see you tomorrow and find out what was going on tonight out there in the park?"

To be honest, I was glad things had worked out the way they had. This would give me time to decide what I would tell Troy about the whole situation. I agreed to talk to him the next day.

I didn't get up the next day till noon---something very unusual for me! I always felt like I had wasted half the day if I got up past six o'clock.

Terry fed me some lunch, and I knew she was dying to know what had taken place the previous evening also. But not wanting to tire me, she didn't ask, especially knowing

Troy probably would be here soon and she could hear it then.

Upon finishing my lunch, I dragged myself to my easy chair, called Troy and made arrangements to see him at four o'clock that afternoon. I tried then to rest with my feet propped up in retirement style.

But now I found myself too awake to snooze or nap, so I reached over and grabbed my books to pursue, even in this relaxed fashion, my study. It took a few minutes for the cobwebs to clear my brain, but soon I was thinking clearly on I Thessalonians 5:12-13.

12 And we beseech you, brethren, to know them who labor among you, and are over you in the Lord, and admonish you,   13 And to esteem them very highly in love for their work's sake.

Initially I noted several thoughts from the verse:

1. The word elder, bishop or pastor is not mentioned in these verses, but the passage does refer to those placed in leadership over the church.

2. There are several verbal ideas in this passage inter-related with several other verbal thoughts:

   a. the believers are to know
           those who labor among them
           those who are over them in the Lord
           those who admonish them

   b. the believers are to esteem these leaders
           very highly for their works' sake

I noted that one Greek article governed the participles translated above as those who labor among them, those who are over them and those who admonish them, indicating that these words speak of several functions of one office.

I noted again that I needed further definitions of these verbal ideas, so I pursued them a little further and found the following:

1. <u>to know</u>
   > the verb here (oida) can also mean
   >> to regard with favor

2. <u>to labor</u>
   > the verb here (koriao) can indicate
   >> an intense labor
   >> to be worn and spent with work
   >> to faint from wearisome labor
   >> to toil
   >> to labor hard

3. <u>to be over</u>
   > the verb (proistemi) has a variety of meanings
   >> to set before
   >> to give prominence
   >> to set over
   >> to exhibit publicly
   >> to chose as one's leader
   >> to put one forward with authority
   >> to appoint with authority
   >> to prefer
   >> to value before another
   >> to establish a thing before another
   >> to preside

to govern
to superintend
to direct

it is the same word as used in other verses
Romans 12:8
I Thessalonians 5:12
I Timothy 3:4
I Timothy 3:5
I Timothy 3:12
I Timothy 5:17
Titus 3:8
Titus 3:14

4. <u>To admonish</u>
to warn
to bring or put in remembrance

5. <u>to esteem highly</u>
this translation reflects a verb and an adverb
the verb---egeomai
to take the lead
to preside
to govern
to think
to consider
to count
to esteem
to regard

the adverb---huperekperissou
in a super abundance
beyond all measure

Thus, I would indicate the meaning of the verse to be as follows:

> The brethren at Thessalonica
>> they must regard leaders with great appreciation
>>> those who are toiling hard in their midst
>>> those who are set over them by the Lord
>>> those who are admonishing them
>> they are to esteem them
>>> with love
>>> above all measure
>>> because of what they do

I further concluded:

1. The above words refer to the same office, not several different offices.

2. The office most clearly indicated by the duties expressed here is the office of the elder/bishop.

3. Some of the characteristics and responsibilities of the office are indicated

    a. they are set in the position by the Lord
    b. they are set over the Thessalonians
        in the place of leadership
        in the place of authority
    c. they are to admonish the members of the body

4. Some of the responsibilities of the members of the body are indicated also:

    a.   they are to regard their leaders with appreciation
    b.   they are to esteem them with love above all
          measure because of the work they do

Thus, the elders or bishops are set by the Lord in a position of leadership and authority in the church, but that is not to say they are to be little two-bit, tin-horn dictators or power-mongering worldlings. If they are to be appreciated and esteemed by the people with a love beyond measure, it will be because of the difficult and spiritual work they do with a love and sensitivity towards the people. There is the possibility that the membership may not treat leaders with the right respect or attitude, but there is also the possibility the leaders may not do their labor in a correct manner or with a proper attitude. Blessed is the church that has both elders and members working together according to these standards, and cursed is the church where these standards are ignored by either party, the elders or members, or by both.

Somewhere about three o'clock I unintentionally drifted off to sleep, but Terry woke me up about thirty minutes later so I could be ready for Troy's visit.

As I tidied up my weak body, I realized I still wasn't sure how much of the story I was going to tell him!

32

Did I Desire a Good Work....?

At four o'clock sharp Troy was at the door. I invited him in, and we talked briefly for a few minutes, and I am sure it was obvious I was nervous. Maybe he thought it was my exhausted condition.

"Troy, did you search the swimming pool area Saturday night after we left?" I began . "And did you find a body?"

"Yes, we searched the area, but we found nothing. Pastor Ira, what was going on the other night? I've almost burnt up my brain trying to figure this one out!"

"I was supposed to meet Phil Millow that night at the swimming pool," I admitted.

"Phil Millow?" he exclaimed.

"Yes, do you know Phil Millow?" I asked somewhat puzzled.

"Not till the other night!" he explained.

"Where did you meet him the other night?" I asked continuing my probe.

"We arrested him that night several hours before your experience in the park!" he declared.

"What for?" I queried in amazement.

"For a crime he is supposed to have committed almost ten years ago," he declared again.

"What crime?" I continued, feeling like a lawyer interrogating a witness.

"For murder!" he shockingly declared again.

"Whose murder?"

"Oh, probably someone you never knew---a fellow named Jim Collier!"

"Was that Mandy Collier's husband?" I asked as I traced the shock in his face.

"Preacher, do you know Mandy Collier?" he demanded. "How in the world do you know her---she is this city's definition of reprobate."

At this point I knew I had to tell him the whole story. I shared that Phil Millow was the one trying to kill him, the one also who had shot me instead. I told him he was acting for Mandy Collier, but I didn't know why. I told him we had almost gotten the reason out of him when we witnessed to him, but Mandy walked in and tore the place apart. I informed him that Phil had called later and offered to tell me the whole story, including why Mandy wanted to kill him. I told him it was Phil Millow I was supposed to meet in the park at the swimming pool, so he could tell me the whole story. I admitted I had been suspicious of Phil's motive to see me, and that maybe he had lured me to the park to kill me too.

I stopped a second or two to get my breath and let him interact if he so desired, but he said nothing.

"So that was why I was in the park," I continued. "That's why I was frightened when you pulled up in your squad car, which I couldn't recognize because of your lights and spotlight. I thought you might be Phil. Then when I saw it was you, I told you to get down because I thought Phil might be in the bushes or somewhere close by waiting to shoot you or me or both. That's why we drove out slouching in the car---lest we might get shot driving away. And now it turns out we had nothing to fear---Phil was already in jail accused of a crime he probably never committed.   And that's why he never showed up for our meeting."

At this point, though Troy's jaw was drooping from shock, he asked a question.

"How do you know he didn't commit that crime almost ten years ago?"

"Because he told me Mandy had ruled his life for almost ten years by threatening to frame him for a crime he hadn't committed.   And I guess, when she found out he was going to tell me everything, including why she wanted you dead, she pulled the rug on him and turned in the evidence against him which she had been keeping for years."

"What a mess!" Troy correctly observed.

"Well that's not all of it.   Phil used to be a preacher and a pastor, and that's where he met Mandy---at his church. He left the ministry, his family and everything for her.   And as Dink would say, that was a bum decision!"

"Preacher, what can we do about it now?" he asked.

By this time my body and brain were worn out again.   I suggested we both think on the subject, and talk about the possibilities and necessities, and talk about the action we had to take the next day.

After supper that night, I napped for about an hour. Feeling rested and restless, I turned to my pursuit, as I now realized it had become an escape from the experiences of the past days.   What a joy that I could forget Phil and Mandy and guns and bullets and jail and hospitals for a few minutes by simply burying myself in thought over this issue. It had become important for more than one reason.

My verse of meditation for a few moments before going to bed was I Timothy 3:1, which read:

This is a true saying, If a man desire the office of a bishop, he desires a good work.

After what I had been going through these past few days, I told Terry that I wondered about this verse. I told her jokingly that I was not sure I had desired the office, nor was I sure it was a good work.

And, yes, I was only kidding. I had desired to be a preacher. I had desired to be a pastor. I hadn't known very much about this matter of elder (episkopos) when I had those desires.

I concluded that maybe this was part of the problem of the church today. Men want to be preachers and what they call a pastor, but they do not realize what it is to be a bishop. This was not to say that the pastor was a bishop---I had not established that yet. It was to say, men desired more the opportunity of ministering before men than they did the hard work of ministering in the background (I remembered I Thessalonians 5:12-13).

But the text clearly declared that a man could desire the office of an elder or overseer, and when he did he was desiring a good work.

As I closed my study, I asked God to give me that kind of a heart---one that was devoted to and longing after the office of a true Biblical overseer of God's people, not for my glory. I asked also for a heart that realized this work was a good work, though it had many trials, tears and disappointments.

33

What Do We Do Next....?

The next day was Saturday, and I was free from sermon preparation again for just one more Sunday, so it was supposed to be a relaxing and peaceful Saturday. My mind was still a little scrambled from the past few days, but I was seriously considering trying to see Phil Millow before the day was over.

When after breakfast I felt somewhat stronger, I called Troy to inquire what he thought would be best. As he spoke, I saw that I agreed with him.

"Pastor, I think you are right---someone needs to see Phil soon, but I'm not sure I am the right one to go with you. Why don't you take Dink, since he was with you when you visited Phil in his home, plus Dink knows his way around the jail."

"That's for sure," I said with a laugh.

Thus, it was decided I would go, taking Dink with me that Saturday afternoon, to try to get to the bottom of why Phil had been trying to kill Troy. Plus, we would leave a witness with him concerning his spiritual condition.

After calling Dink, that left the morning free so I turned again to my study of elders. I marveled at the time I had been able to give to this search, time that God in His providence had given through all of the unpredictable and uninvited circumstances. What a marvelous sovereign God I served.

My verses for study this day were I Timothy 3:2-7.

2 A bishop then must be blameless, the husband of one wife, vigilant, sober, of good behavior, given to hospitality, apt to teach;
3 Not given to wine, no striker, not greedy of filthy lucre, but patient, not a brawler, not covetous;
4 One that ruleth well his own house, having his children in subjection with all gravity.
5 (For if a man know not how to rule his own house, how shall he take care of the church of God?);
6 Not a novice, lest being lifted up with pride he fall into condemnation of the devil.
7 Moreover, he must have a good report of them who are without, lest he fall into reproach and the snare of the devil.

I gave a sigh of relief when I had finished reading that passage---what a list of qualifications! I wondered how many churches or even elders took them seriously!

I sat back for a few moments wanting to consider them for a while as I also saw the individual requirements included therein. I made the following observations contemplating the list in this manner.

1. The elders were to be men, as clearly seen by the requirement that the elder was to be the husband of one wife. Couple that with all the other verses on elders (both Old and New Testaments), and there is no evidence or grounds for women serving as elders. And again, link these thoughts with the

total Biblical teaching of man as the leader in the home as well as in the church, and the above conclusion seems clear.

2. The elders were to be mature and godly men, not beginners or even older men who were chosen to serve as elders only because they were successful in other areas of life.

3. The elders were to be leaders, for it is stated they are not qualified to lead the church if they are unable to superintend their own houses.

4. The elders were to be beyond reproach in their lives and character as evidenced in the various moral requirements:

    a. unblameable in their married lives
    b. unblameable in their seriousness of mind
    c. unblameable in their chaste living
    d. unblameable in their temperance toward wine
    e. unblameable in their reasonableness
    f. unblameable in the reactions towards disputes
    g. unblameable in their attitude toward money
    h. unblameable in their home lives
    i. unblameable in their spiritual warfare
    j. unblameable in their reputation before the world

About this time in my study, someone began knocking on the front door. Terry answered it, and in came Dink, urging me to get dressed so we could visit the jail. He had found out the best visitation time was at 11:00 in the morning---just about forty-five minutes away. I threw on my clothes, and we were on our way.

I had hoped to have a few minutes of meditation before we had to go to the jail, which would have been the case had we gone in the afternoon. Now as we drove, I tried to form a plan of approach and questioning when I faced Phil. Little did I realize then, that all my plans were unnecessary in light of what we would face at the jail.

34

Do I know You Guys....?

When we arrived at the local jail, Dink was beside himself, as he joked and greeted everyone from the custodians to the inmates. As several doors slammed behind us, he sobered somewhat as he declared, "Preacha, sure glad God saved me from all dis!"

After we came to a waiting area, we did just that--- waited for someone to bring Phil to us. But he never came out! The officer in charge said Phil claimed he didn't know either one of us! Understandably we were very disappointed. We had hoped to get to the bottom of this mystery once and for all.

Dink was more upset than I was.

"How he eva gonna tell us what we wants to know if he don't see us?" he stated almost demandingly.

He began to rattle off in a whisper to me several plans whereby we could make him talk eventually---everything from flattery to pressure by some of his old friends, who would be serving time with Phil once he hit the "big house," as Dink called it---his description of the state penitentiary.

I tried to explain to him that God had His ways and didn't need "da Dink's help." He finally settled down as we walked out the last clanging door and made it to our car. And he finally saw it.

"Yeah," he said, "I guess I'm still learnin that sovernty stuff---God is sovern and He will put da pressure on old

Phil, or whatever He wants to do in da sitiation. Boy, dat's a great doctrine!"

As I drove home, I could only wonder what had changed Phil's mind. Twice he was going to tell me why Mandy wanted Troy dead, and even a third time, but now he had refused. Our disappointment was obvious as neither of us said much as we drifted through the streets of Collegetown.

I was so disappointed when I got home, though I had committed it to the Lord, I didn't want to see any one, talk to any one, or mess with any one the rest of the day. But isn't that just the time we "fall into various trials?" Sitting in my easy chair was none other than Todd---looking like a man who had just found a million dollars.

"Hey, Ira!" he bellowed with his old boyish grin. "Have I got news for you!"

I remembered the last time I had seen him. He was moaning and groaning about how horrible elder rule at Middleville Baptist appeared to be. What could possibly have happened to bring such a change? I decided to try to pull an answer out of him.

"Well, you're awfully chipper today! What has put your soul on happy street, especially since our last visit?" I asked with a smile.

"Ira, I'm getting married!"

"What? When? And who is she?" I stumbled in unbelief.

"You don't know her---but she's a beauty---just what God ordered for me!" he crowed.

"How do you know God ordered her for you?" I asked with some sarcasm.

"Well, the elders confirmed it to me," he boasted confidently.

I had two questions for him.

"You mean you are still at Middleville?" I asked. To which he answered with a yes.

Then came my second question, since I saw no reason to argue over that decision after our previous discussion.

"Did they confirm it to you, or did you confirm it to them?" I asked with some suspicion.

"Well, they told me she was the girl I was to marry (even though I had never met her) before I could leave, and that if I rejected God's will on the job there at Middleville, I would also miss God's will for my life in marriage. I must admit, at first I was full of unbelief. But after much prayer, and with their counsel, I finally agreed to meet her. Then when I saw her and talked to her, I submitted to the will of God on the matter, agreeing to stay on the job and to marry her. And, boy, I've never been happier."

"You mean they planned for you to marry her before you ever met her?" I queried with dismay.

"Well, yes, but I have learned from this that one must trust the judgment of the elders, and obey them in all matters," he excusingly declared. "That's what the Bible says!" he proclaimed confidently.

"Where?" I asked bluntly.

"Oh, Ira, why can't you rejoice with me in this hour, instead of trying to start a theological argument or discussion? Billy Motley said you wouldn't like our decision!"

I wanted to say, "Is Billy Motley playing Holy Spirit in your life now? What will he ask you to do next which you must obey without question?"

But I throttled my tongue and said with boldness, "Todd, you had better be sure this is God's will for your life or it will be a catastrophe---a major catastrophe which could wreck your life and your ministry! I wouldn't be surprised to hear she was a daughter of one of the elders!"

His reply was a lengthy one, and though revealing, not convincing.

"Ira, I must admit that I was upset when I first went to be Billy Motley's assistant pastor. I thought they were too legalistic, gave the elders too much power, and would make too many decisions in my life. But I came to see that they had only my best interest at heart. I have learned more there, have been more submitted to the Lord, and more certain of His will for my life than ever before. Now, don't you try to play Holy Spirit in my life. I am not under your authority, but under the authority of the elders of Middleville Baptist Church, and if we see this to be the will of God for my life, I am submissive to it. What difference does it make if she is the daughter of one of the elders?"

It was obvious no one could change his mind, so I gave up trying. I only hoped he would not live to regret this decision, but I had to admit I was not hopeful in the matter.

I was glad when he left---glad to get my easy chair back, and glad to sit and do nothing this Saturday afternoon and evening. I was not even tempted to open my thoughts on the subject of elders!

35

Are There Several Kinds of Elders....?

After resting the Lord's day, the last Sunday I was determined to be absent from my pulpit, I decided to rest Monday also before easing into the week.

Rest, though I decided, would include a return to my study on elders. My next verse of consideration was I Timothy 5:17:

Let the rulers that rule well be counted worthy of double honor, especially they who labor in word and doctrine.

I made several notes on my study sheet:

1. The Greek word for rulers is presbuteroi (the plural of presbuteros) or elders.

2. The word for rule is proistemi (a word we had seen before in our study), and it means to govern, to preside, or to superintend.

3. The word for well is kalos, an adverb, meaning rightly or correctly.

4. The phrase "be counted worthy" means to be esteemed worthy or to be esteemed as deserving or to be recognized highly.

5. The word for honor means dignity or value or worth. Thus, the elders who govern, preside or superintend are to be esteemed worthy of double honor or double dignity or double respect.

6. But there is another kind of elder besides the one who leads God's people---the one laboring or being spent or wearied in word and doctrine, that is, in preaching or teaching.

I now noted several observations from these thoughts:

1. I asked as before, where is the mention of the deacons in this group of leaders in the church? I again had to conclude the implication was that the deacons were not part of the presiding or governing leadership of the church.

2. I had to admit that there are two kinds of elders--- those leading God's people and those who teach God's people the word or doctrine.

3. I asked again how these who teach the word or doctrine were to be related to the office of the pastor/teacher. These seemed clearly to be the same office---elders who were pastor/teachers, who were given the responsibility of ministering the Word of God to the people of God.

4. The remaining question was whether this was
    one office (elders) with two functions (ruling
    and teaching) or two offices (ruling elders and
    teaching elders). I decided quickly to pursue
    this question in my next study.

5. For now it was clear from this verse that both
    elders who rule and the elders who teach are
    worthy of great respect, but the teaching
    elders were to be given even a greater respect.

Though it was unwelcome, the phone invaded my
thoughts at this moment. I answered with less than an
enthusiastic attitude, but the message soon jerked me out of
my meditative study.

"Rev. Pointer? This is the jail. Mr. Phil Millow, one of
our inmates, wants to see you. Could you visit him this
afternoon?"

I felt like replying that I had been there just Saturday,
and he had refused to see me. But too much was at stake
for such a reply.

"Yes, I'll be there about one o'clock."

"He has requested that you come alone!"

I reminded myself that I had heard that one before also!
I wondered if I was really going to get to see him, and if so,
would he give me the truth?

And I had thought this was going to be a day of rest...?

36

Why Are You Trying to Kill Troy....?

As I left the house to drive to the jail, my mind wondered how many more times I would get my hopes raised by Phil Millow, only to have them dashed to pieces by his change of mind. But as one who believed in prayer, and because I had been praying, I went with hope one more time.

When I finally sat face to face with him, it was obvious he was suffering deeply. But I asked him about his health any way. He looked the other way, as if he didn't want to talk about it. He finally acknowledged that his health was the least of his worries.

I had decided to let him guide the conversation and tell me what was on his mind, and it didn't take him long to get to the subject.

"Preacher, I'm sorry I couldn't make it to the park the other night. I really intended to be there, but I was arrested before I got there. And then when I got thrown into jail, I went into a tailspin and didn't want to see any one. I thought it would only make matters worse for me. I am sorry!"

I gave him a noncommittal nod, and let him continue. But I wasn't ready for the next statement and not necessarily because of its abruptness.

"Preacher, I have been trying to kill Troy for Mandy because she is his real mother!"

"What?" I exclaimed in pure reaction. "Repeat that!"

"Mandy Collier is Troy Medford's real mother!" he repeated.

"But I thought he was a Medford," I mumbled in amazement.

"So does he and so does every one else. But he's not a Medford! He's a Collier. His father is the one I am accused of killing. But the one who really killed him was Mandy. The Medford family adopted him when Mandy gave him up for adoption when he was born."

"But how does that explain why she is trying to kill him now?" I asked, searching for the logic of a mother having such an attitude toward her own child?

"She never wanted him. She didn't want to give birth to him. She never wanted him to live. She wanted to have him aborted, but that was before the days of legal abortion. She illegally aborted a child earlier, and it just about killed her, so she didn't want to take another chance on that line of action. But now that abortion is legal, she figures in her reprobate mind she has the right to kill him. She argues, "What is the difference whether she killed him in the womb or after he's born?"

Strangely enough, I had to agree with one part of her twisted logic---there's no difference between killing a baby in the womb and killing a person in adulthood. But I would use the argument for not killing the baby or the adult, and she would use the argument for killing either or both.

"Preacher," he continued, "how could I ever have been fooled by her, and why did I continue to do her dirty work, even to the point of attempted murder?"

"You said attempted murder?" I asked.

"Yes, attempted murder! Preacher, I never killed any one! And the Lord kept me from killing Troy. But my life is such a mess!"

We continued to talk for another hour or so. But we didn't discuss the subject of murder. We talked about his life and God's grace and mercy to sinners. We covered his conversion experience---whether it was a true one or not. We poured over Scripture. We wept---he because of his sin and I because I saw deeper than ever in my life the miserable devastating power of sin in the life of a believer.

Here was a man that had left his sacred calling, his loving wife, his precious children, a promising future in the ministry, a church that loved him, and a joy only Christ could give. And for what?---nothing and even less than nothing. I also saw the power and deception of the enemy.

Then finally we prayed together. He cried to God from the depth of his soul. He recalled the past days of blessing and pled with God to restore them. He writhed in the anguish of repentance. Then he thanked God for his restoration. Then I prayed, but could hardly speak as I too choked back the tears.

Not a word was spoken about getting him out of jail. In fact, he asked me to pray that he could be a witness to others around him even as Paul had been during his imprisonment.

I promised him I would be back soon, and we could talk about his future. His reply was encouraging.

"Preacher, I don't care if I have to stay in jail the rest of my life, because now I am truly free. Better to be free in the Lord and in jail, than out of jail and enslaved in the spirit of the enemy!"

My spirit was soaring in the heavenlies when I left the jail. God had done a marvelous work! But there were still problems to face.

How would I share this information with Troy?

How could I witness to Mandy?

What was next for Phil?

And the lesser question, but still important----where am I now in my study of church government?

Three Offices or Two Offices....?

As I arrived home that Monday evening, I was almost oblivious to the time. I hadn't even looked at my wristwatch or the clock in the car. My mind had been spinning over the torrent of events sweeping over me. As we ate supper, I shared the afternoon's events and information with Terry.

After supper, though it was difficult, I returned to my meditation on church government. I found in the notes from my last study that I needed to decide if the New Testament set forth two offices (elders and deacons) or three offices (elders, deacons and pastor/teachers).

The Scriptures gave qualifications for elders and deacons, as I had seen in I Timothy 3, so obviously there were at least two offices.

But what about the pastor/teacher of Ephesians 4:11? Was this a separate office making three offices, or was this the same as the teacher/elder of I Timothy 5:17? And even if this was the teacher/elder, could there not be three offices in the church?

I pushed back in my lounge chair for a few moments to think. What did we really have here if there were three offices in the church? I thought of the duties stated for each:

Deacons

The very meaning of the word for deacon was servant. They were never in the New Testament given the duty of leadership or rule, nor the function of ministering to God's people, though some had ministered. They were servant ministers.

Elders

They were the shepherds and spiritual leaders of the church. Their duties were two-fold---to lead and govern the church, on one hand, and also, on the other hand, to minister the Word of God. Thus, there were ruling and teaching elders.

Pastor/Teachers

These were men specially gifted to minister the Word of God. These were the second group of elders.

As I sat there I asked myself where I might get some direction on this matter in the Word of God. Then I remembered the unity of the Bible, and the light I had received from the Old Testament earlier in my study on the subject.

So I asked the simple question: Did the same men in the Old Testament minister the Word of God? That is, did the elders in the Old Testament teach and minister the Word of God to the people? Then the answer hit me like a bolt of lightning! The answer was no!

The elders represented the people in the Old Testament for the purpose of leadership, rule and judgment of moral and civil matters. They were not ministers of the Word of

God to the people. There was another office for the ministry of the Word---the office of the priesthood.

At this point I grabbed my pen and began taking notes as I remembered the previous study. I recorded that there was no clear or certain change in offices as one moved from the Old Testament to the New Testament church. The elders emerge in the New Testament unannounced, giving a silent conclusion that there was the existence in the new covenant of elders as there had been in the old covenant.

If that were the case, I asked myself if this Old Testament separation of rule (elders) and ministry of the Word (the Levites or the priesthood) had ever in the New Testament been changed or re-fashioned, and I had to conclude the answer was no.

I did note that the term "elder" was a very broad term in the New Testament and included apostles, rulers and ministers of the Word. I also concluded that not all elders were apostles (that was obvious), and on that basis neither should I conclude that the indication that ministers were elders should force the conclusion that all elders were ministers in the New Testament church, or that there was a single office of elder in the church.

I remembered also from my study of this very subject that Paul makes a distinction between the gifts of ruling and teaching in passages such as Romans 12:4-8 and I Corinthians 12:1-31.

My final conclusions began to emerge:

1. There are three offices in the New Testament church---deacons, elders and pastor/teachers.

2. The deacon is involved in servant ministry, concerning the material needs of the church.

3. The elder has the primary duty of leadership
    or spiritual rule.

4. The pastor/teacher is an elder, but a very unique
    kind of elder---even a different office, though he
    is an elder. His responsibility is the ministry of
    the Word of God.

5. The pastor/teacher is the spiritual leader, also of
    the body of elders, since he is the man who is in
    the Word and most knowledgeable of the Word.
    His gifts lie in the ability to study the Word, speak
    the Word, and apply the Word to the life of the
    church. Who else in the congregation would be
    more qualified to lead the elders than this pastor/
    teacher? And would it not be contradictory to give
    one man the gift and duty of speaking and applying
    the Word of God, but then separate that gift from
    the guidance of those responsible to rule the church?
    Obviously, this is not to say the pastor/teacher is a
    dictator of the elders, any more than to say the
    elders are dictators of the people. But it is to say
    that one individual must have the reins of
    leadership. A congregation cannot be led by a
    multitude of men who have the same authority,
    with none of them given the place of primary
    leadership, any more than one could have a multi-
    headed animal.

An air of triumph came over my soul as I felt I had
come through a major break-through. The greatest
problems I could imagine in a church could come from

either everyone being in charge or rule of the church (congregational rule) or no one being in charge of the primary leadership of the church (a body of elders with no one having the primary responsibility of leadership).

How much better to follow the Scriptural pattern of a body of elders, which would include a gifted pastor/teacher or gifted pastor/teachers to lead even the elders in their labors to lead the church! Even then, one pastor/teacher would need to lead the other pastor/teachers.

38

What Did You Say....?

As I went to bed that Monday evening, I was reminded that the day had contained two break-throughs. One was in the case regarding Troy, and the other was in the pursuit of my chosen subject.

I was also reminded that the Troy situation was not finished. I had to try to see Mandy, and I had to tell Troy who she was, although I had no idea what approach to take. I determined to sleep on it (it was too late in the evening anyway), and then plot my strategy in the morning.

But I was unexpectedly awakened from my sleep about three o'clock in the morning. The voice on the other end of the phone was Phil Millow. He was deeply disturbed!

"Preacher, Mandy just shot herself---she's dead!"

"What did you say?" I asked trying to shake the cobwebs from my brain.

"I said, Mandy just committed suicide!"

"Where?" I responded, showing I was finally in the thinking world.

"At her house. Preacher, she called me just after you left yesterday afternoon. I tried to witness to her, telling her of my new joy in Christ---assuring her I was finished with her and the life of sin we had been living. I even told her you knew about her relationship to Troy. I tried to share the gospel with her in humility and love, but she wouldn't listen. She kept cursing me, the Lord, you, and

Dink, but especially Troy. Finally, she hung up on me. Then about ten minutes ago, they woke me up here in jail and told me she was dead---she had killed herself. She blew her head off with a shotgun!"

I sank into my chair with a sigh of relief and sorrow. But he spoke again.

"Preacher, the one who responded to the police call, when the neighbors heard a shot and reported it, was Troy! It seems he found his own mother dead, but didn't know who she was. He looked upon her as just another corpse!"

"Did any one tell him who she was?" I asked with great concern.

"No, as far as I know, no one knew but you and me and Mandy---and she never told him."

I thanked him, hung up, and then debated my next move. I figured it would take the police awhile to clean up the bloody scene, so I thought I might go there. Then I wondered what good that would do. Troy would want to know why I was there, and what reason could I give except the truth---but was he ready for the truth? I decided to let him get his work finished, go off duty, get his rest, and then see him later in the day away from the suicide scene, and try to explain it all to him.

As I stretched back out on the bed and pulled the covers up around me, I fearfully marveled at the depravity of the human heart, and the power of the enemy to capture and dominate a soul which rejects the grace of God, surrenders to him, and is willing to serve him. What seeds there are in the human heart by nature---hatred so great that one would desire to kill one's own child; stubbornness and deceit so great one would seek to frame some one else for a crime he did not commit; and even the insanity of self-destruction. Oh, the power of the enemy to enslave an individual to contradict even the most basic human yearning of self-preservation. If not for God's grace, would we not all follow this road, evidencing in some manner the full potential of our sin.

Yes, and even in the believer there remained the remnants of sin as evidenced in Phil Millow. Then I saw a relationship between these events and my subject of church government. I realized that even saved men, who are leading the church, can appear to be walking in righteousness, while being unconsciously or consciously driven by self-interest, pride, thirst for control over others, and similar areas of their remnants of depravity.

The conclusion was surely that there must be some accountability for the elders and pastor-teacher in light of the subtle but definite reality of human depravity. Not even godly men could be given complete and unbridled authority over the people of God in light of the power of sin to deceive the human heart (even the heart of an elder), and in turn, the power of sin to lead to the practice of hypocrisy from such a deceived heart (even again in the heart of an elder). Could any one be more prone and more expert to take the office of an elder and turn it toward legalism, manipulation, and ruination of the church and the people of God?

I finally fell off to sleep marveling that these two events (the suicide and the study on church government) had in the sovereignty of God actually culminated in a valuable spiritual lesson.

39

What Shall I Tell Troy...?

I didn't sleep well the rest of that night. I was racked by mixed emotions---elated over my study, but uncertain of what to say to Troy. I knew I would probably have to face him the next day.

Sure enough, the phone call came rather early the next morning!

"Brother Ira, I hope I'm not calling too early," he began. I smiled remembering I had used that line before in trying to soften a phone call before the roosters got up.

I told him I had been through a bad night, but that I was awake nonetheless.

Then he came to the subject, and I understood fully why he was calling so early.

"Preacher, have you heard that Mandy Collier is dead!"

"Yes, Phil called me last night, told he she committed suicide, and that's why I was sleeping a little later than usual."

"Have you heard I was sent to the death scene to clean up the mess?" he continued in a very serious tone.

I wondered if he knew something!

"Preacher, some one just called the station here as I was checking out and said that Mandy Collier was my mother! What a crazy idea! Then I called Phil in jail, and he said to call you! Do you know anything about that?"

Wow! I did a double-take on that one in a hurry. I wondered if he suspected me of hiding information from him. Then I asked him a question so I could stall for a few minutes.

"Have you addressed your familly with that question?"

"No, I haven't. For one thing, its too early in the morning. Besides that, I feel closer to you than to my family since what happened at First Baptist Church, and since I followed you in leaving there to help start Unity Baptist Church."

Now it was back squarely in my lap! I couldn't dodge the question any longer.

"Troy, meet me at the Sunshine Cafe, and I'll tell you what I know. I'll be there in fifteen minutes!"

He agreed, and I began to scramble both physically and mentally to get ready for our apointment.

When we met at the cafe, I told him the whole story--- who she was, why she had been trying to kill him, including the fact she was his mother. I expected him to cry or show some emotion, but he didn't. He just sat listening and asking an ocassional question with a blank stare on his face. I apologized for not telling him sooner, but explained I didn't know how to approach the subject.

He seemed to understand, but it had shaken him deeply, even though the emotions were pent up inside.

He finally asked, "How am I supposed to react to the news that a woman I only knew from a distance, a woman who was full of wickedness, a woman who would have aborted me at birth if she could have, a woman who was trying to kill me, a woman who is now dead, a woman whose suicide I was called to investigate, was my mother? Should I rejoice I never knew her? Should I be glad I never had to grow up in her home? Should I thank God He spared me her influence? Should I be jumping up and down with praise that I didn't know this until she's dead? Or should I feel sorrow that my biological mother is dead, and I never knew that fact while she was alive? Am I to go through life thinking maybe I could have helped her had I known?"

I decided I was not going to answer those questions. How much better for one to come to his own conclusions, than for me to try to convince him of my own.

So I asked, "What do you think the Bible says? What is God's answer here?"

He looked meditatively down at the table for a long time, wrinkled his face and lip to fight off a breakdown, and then he answered.

"The Bible answer is that God is sovereign! He is sovereign even over sin, sorrow, losses, apparent failures, yea, every event and circumstance of life."

With that clear answer from him, I decided to help him on the next question he was facing.

"Amen, God is sovereign, even over your birth and life, and all the circumstances even today, including Mandy's attitude toward you, and yea, her death. But that doesn't mean you are wrong to feel sorrow! God was sovereign over the death of His own Son, but He grieved over the event and the sin of those who planned and carried it out. So weep if you wish, grieve as you must, but from your tears and sorrow praise God for His providential ways."

I quoted for him a poem I used often in times of sorrow:

My Father's way may twist and turn,
My heart may throb and ache,
But in my soul, I'm glad I know,
God maketh no mistake!

We closed our conversation and parted, with Troy seeming to have gained a victory. I thought I was now moving away from the Mandy Collier event, but it was not quite finished, as I discovered when I arrived home.

Will You Preach a Funeral....?

The message awaiting me, when I arrived at home late in the morning, was from one of the local funeral parlors, wanting to know if I would preach Mandy Collier's funeral. They said her husband, Phil Millow, had made the request, to which I agreed.

But that was not the only surprise at home. Todd had called and wanted to bring his fiancee by so Terry and I could meet her. I called him back and agreed to see them later in the afternoon, even though I had my hands full.

Then after resting a little while, I turned to my beloved study of church government. I was nearing the end now, but still had a few more verses to consider to see if they added anything to my conclusions so far. I decided to take them in one fell swoop.

Titus 1:5-9

Still considering them in the order in which they appear in the Bible, the first passage was Titus 1:5-9. Part of the text was clearly parallel to the I Timothy 3 passage which covered the qualifications of the elders. The passage indicated the following:

verse 5

Paul left Titus in Crete so he might do two things:
(1) correct the things lacking, and (2) ordain elders
in every city as Paul had commanded him. This
verse seemed to indicate again a plurality of elders
in each city as we had seen previously.

verses 6-9

Paul states the qualifications for elders once again:
an elder is to be
irreproachable
faithful in marriage,
having faithful children,
without any accusation of profligacy or
lawlessness
unblameable as a steward of God
not willful
not prone to anger
not given to wine
not quarrelsome
not eager for dishonorable gain
hospitable
a lover of virtue
one of sound mind
one who is righteous
one who is devout or holy
one who has mastered self
one holding firmly to true doctrine so he can
persuade others by sound doctrine
and refute opposition

I noted again that the terms elder (presbuteros) and overseer (episkopos) were used interchangeably as we had seen previously.

Hebrews 13:7

This verse read as follows:

Remember them who have the rule over you, who have spoken unto you the word of God, whose faith follow, considering the end of their conversation of life.

My observations were again as follows:

1. The believers have a responsibility
    to the ones leading or ruling them
    to the ones speaking to them the Word of God

2. The believers' responsibility is two-fold
    to remember or be mindful of them
    to imitate their faith
        beholding attentively their conduct

Thus, there are those who lead or rule the church. Though the word elder is not used here, this probably refers to the elders. The elders should also lead or rule by the speaking (preaching and teaching) of the Word of God. The believers should be mindful of their work (show respect and love and appreciation, something we have seen in previous verses), and seek to imitate their faith by watching their conduct very attentively. This also indicates the elders should be very careful how they live, in light of the fact the church members are watching their holiness of life or lack thereof. Thus, what the elders do should be Biblical.

It seems also that there is an indication in this verse that the elders should be accountable. What if they do not live holy and godly lives? Will they not lead astray the believers who should be watching them attentively and seeking to imitate them? Should not the church therefore have a standard of accountability, and a means of members holding the elders to that standard of accountability?

I remembered I Timothy 5:19-20 at this point, which indicates again the elders must be held accountable:

> *19 Against an elder receive not an accusation, but before two or three witnesses.   20 Them that sin rebuke before all, that others may fear.*

My exegetical notes recorded the following nuances:

1. Receive---a present imperative, thus a command
2. Accusation---a crimination (accusation of a crime or sin)
3. before two or three witnesses---this could be either before two or three witnesses or by two or three witnesses
4. rebuke---another imperative meaning to convict, expose, reprove, rebuke, or discipline

Thus, the church is commanded not to receive an accusation of wrong-doing against an elder except it be brought by two or more witnesses. When it has been established as true, the elder is to be disciplined before the church so that others may be given a holy fear of God, and see the sorrow and danger of sin.

Here were the verses I had been seeking! These verses devastated any idea that the elders are above challenge and accountability except before God. The church has the right and the duty to hold them accountable. It can never be that they are above any scrutiny or question.

The balance is clear: God's people are to be led and ruled by elders who do their work according to the Word of God. God's people are to imitate them as they live by the Word of God which they speak. If they do not speak and live the Word of God, the people of God have the right and obligation to bring forward accusations against them, if presented by two or three witnesses. If it is found the elders have sinned, they are to be rebuked before all, so others may see the church takes sin seriously---even the sin of the elders. No man, not even an elder or the elders as a whole, are independent of accountability, answerable only to God.

I thought to myself again, "Any one who believes in man's total depravity ought to understand the necessity to hold the elders accountable and not give to them dictatorial authority and rule over the church!"

I wondered if these verses might help me when I met with Todd in a few moments!

41

Who Is That New Pastor....?

Though I was bone-tired and had no desire to see Todd or his future wife, I made the best effort I could to get ready for them when the hour approached. I could hardly wait, to be honest, to see what kind of girl she was---the elder's daughter and the elders' choice.

At the appointed hour, the expected knock came at the door. I laughed under my breath, because usually Todd was a late arrival. When I opened the door, he was more perky and bubbly than usual. I guessed he was seeking to impress her. She on the other hand hardly said a word, looked somewhat bored, and let him do all the talking.

Terry and I welcomed them both, invited them to sit down on the couch, and sought to engage them in conversation. Then Todd chirped up with a gigantic surprise---yea, a downright explosion.

"Well, Ira, guess what?"

That seemed to be his favorite way to start a conversation, and I had given up a long time ago trying to guess anything about Todd.

"Todd, I have no idea what might come out of your mouth!"

"Well," he said with an airful boast, "you're looking at the pastor of a church now!"

"You're pastoring again. I thought you would be at Middleville Baptist Church for the rest of your life!" I spoke exaggeratingly.

"Yup, I probably will be!" he continued, not coming down off pious mountain one step.

"Do you mean to say that you are pastor of Middleville Baptist Church?" I asked in unbelief.

"Yes sir, as sure as my name is Todd. I am the pastor of Middleville Baptist Church!"

"What happened to the Rev. Billy Motley, the super-know-it-all elder over there?" I asked with some shame and conviction even as the words came out of my mouth.

"The elders fired him!" Todd explained.

"The elders fired him?" I asked dumbfoundedly.

Todd laughed and asked, "Is there an echo in here? Yes the elders fired him, and then asked me to be their pastor!"

Old Todd was enjoying himself as he unveiled this revelation.

"How did that happen?" I continued my questioning.

"Well, one of the elders rose up against him and the others followed. He tried to defend himself, but this elder stood up and faced Billy down in debate. He reminded Billy that he had told and taught them that all elders have the same authority. That meant that Billy had no more leadership authority than any of the other elders. This elder told Billy, 'I'm just like you! I have just as much authority as you! I have just as much leadership in this church as you. I and the other elders have the authority, and if we agree to do so, we can ask you to resign! And we're doing that now!'"

"What did Billy do?" I asked.

"What could he do? He resigned. They were just following the truth which Billy had taught them. All elders are equal. The pastor/teacher is an elder and has no more leadership authority in the church than any other of the ruling elders. This Billy had taught them, and this Billy had to follow in practice, or admit he had taught falsehood, which would have been grounds, they said, for dismissal any way."

"And then you took this church to pastor it?" I said with disgust.

"Yes sir. I look upon it as a great privilege to pastor Middleville Baptist Church."

"But don't you realize that what they did to Billy Motley they can and probably will do to you? Don't you realize that they are using you to get through a crisis, and when the convenient time comes, they will send you packing also?"

"Oh, they'll not treat me that way---I'm marrying one of the elders' daughters---the lead elder who stood up to Billy. He will protect me from the others, won't he dear?" he stated, now trying to bring his future wife into the sad discussion.

I gave up trying to reason with him. He was taking a shaky church for the wrong reasons, without proper procedure, and with a time bomb ticking under his future from day-one. I thought I had seen every thing from Todd in the realm of stupidity, but this topped any thing he had done previously.

As we sat and talked, the phone rang. A muffled indistinct voice addressed me on the line.

"Pastor Pointer, I wonder if I could see you some time soon?"

"Well, yes, I suppose, but who is this?"

"This is Billy Motley, and I must talk to some one!"

42

Who Is Going to Call Me Next....?

I had no desire to see Billy Motley. I hadn't really cared to see Todd and his future wife! I was tired. I was tired of seeing people, talking to people, and trying to help them with their problems!

I knew this had to be a result of near exhaustion again. When would they leave me alone? No one seemed to understand, I needed rest!

Terry seemed to understand where I was, and graciously invited our guests to leave.

"Todd and Jane, it was so good of you to stop by to see us. But this has been a busy day for Ira, and he is still recuperating, you know. I'm afraid I'm going to have to insist he get a nap before supper. I hope you understand."

We exchanged departing pleasantries, and they were gone. I was not impressed with Jane. She seemed moody and unhappy, but I admitted I had not seen her but a few minutes, and Todd had dominated the conversation. Plus, she was not the raving beauty Todd had made her out to be, not that this fact made any difference to me. But it did make me suspect of his motives in agreeing to marry her.

I had not told Todd that it was Billy Motley on the phone. Some things are best left unsaid. I had agreed to see him the next day, only after I had an evening and night of rest!

After a nap and supper, I did feel somewhat better. So I dove into my relaxing pursuit of church government. I was getting close to the end, and was chomping at the bit to share what I had found with the church---just as soon as I was able!

I Peter 5:1-4

The passage read as follows:

1   The elders who are among you I exhort, who am also an elder, and a witness of the sufferings of Christ, and also a partaker of the glory that shall be revealed:
2   Feed the flock of God which is among you, taking the oversight of it, not by constraint but willingly; not for filthy lucre but of a ready mind;
3   Neither as being lords over God's heritage, but being examples to the flock.
4   And when the chief Shepherd shall appear, ye shall receive a crown of glory that fadeth not away.

I divided the passage as follows for my understanding:

I   THE ONE EXHORTING   1

Peter
    the fellow-elder
       sumpresbuteros
    the fellow-partaker
       of the soon-to-be-revealed glory
    the witness
       of the sufferings of Christ

II   THE ONES BEING EXHORTED   2

the elders among those being addressed
   presbuterous

III   THE EXHORTATION OF THE ELDER   2-4

Feed the flock of God among you   2

Feed
   2pl aor[1] imptv act from poimaino meaning
      to feed a flock
      to tend a flock
      to pasture
      to superintend

the flock of God
   God's people
   the local church

among you
   the local church where you are
   the local church where you serve
   the local church where you are appointed

overseeing   2

episkopountes---a nom pl masc pres act part
   from episkopeo
   meaning
      to oversee
      to direct
      to lead or rule

not by constraint but willingly   2

> not unwillingly
> not by compulsion
> not involuntarily
> not by force
> not by duty
> from a willing heart before God
> from a voluntary spirit in the sight of God
> from spontaneous desire in the presence of God

not for filthy lucre but of a ready mind   2

> not for the sake of base gain
> not for the benefit to yourselves
> not eager for dishonorable gain
> not for sordid profit
> but heartily even if no financial reward
> but eagerly even if no personal gain
> but readily even if no profit

neither as being lords over God's heritage   3

> lords---katakurieuontes---nom pl masc pres part
>> from katakurieuo meaning
>>> not as power-mongers
>>> not as domineering leaders
>>> not as grabbers of mastery

> heritage---ton kleron---a gen pl from kleros meaning
>> an assignment
>> an investure
>> an allotment

a part
a portion
a share

but being examples unto the flock   3

examples---tupoi---a nom pl masc from tupos
meaning
a model pattern
an impress
an example

IV THE REWARD FOR THE ELDERS

the time of the reward
when the Chief Shepherd comes
from archipoimenos

the reward
the enduring crown of glory

This passage confirmed what I had been seeing in my past several studies. The elders were to possess the right motive, the right attitude, and the correct goal in doing their work. The admonition to do the work in a certain proper manner, indicated the possibility that the office could be filled by men who would perform it in an improper manner.

Instructions concerning how to deal with corrupt elders or even mistaken elders was not given. But in reality it boiled down to several possibilities, if a Christian or a church found itself with elders doing the work improperly.

1. The Christian or church members could pray and leave the matter in God's hands.

2. The Christian or church members could leave the church and go to another church.

3. The Christian or church members could follow some clearly structured principles of bringing the single or the several accusations even against the elder or elders.

The first option sounds very pious, but how would that really address the grievance and problem? Surely God has given the church the duty of keeping the church pure as we see the many verses on church discipline. I remembered also what I had seen in II Timothy 5:19-20.

The second option does not solve the problem either. It surrenders the church to sin and the improper actions of men who are corrupting the church of the Lord Jesus.

The third option is the proper one. Remember again II Timothy 5:19-20.

By this time I was ready to quit my study. I had pushed myself a little longer than best, but I wanted to finish this section of Scripture. I had been nodding, fighting sleep for about thirty minutes. I finally laid the books aside and crawled into bed. I really wasn't too excited about the next day. I did rejoice over one thing---a few more days and I could go back to work. Maybe I could get a little rest then, and people would leave me alone! But not likely!

43

What Will Rev. Billy Motley Say...?

The next morning I really felt better, but this was the day I had agreed to see Billy Motley. I got up fighting a bitterness in my heart against him over the mess he had made in so many lives. He had spread confusion and arrogance in many places. I had no idea what frame of mind I would find him in on this day. My frame of mind was not good until I had my devotions, and confessed the matter to the Lord, and asked Him for a right attitude.

About 11:00 o'clock I left to have lunch with him as agreed. But when I located him in the restaurant, I never would have recognized him! The arrogance was gone. And it was clear he had learned some lessons from his sad experience.

He confided in me that he realized now he had created a monster at Middleville Baptist Church when he led them into elder rule. It was not that elder rule was unscriptural, but the way in which he instituted it in the church. He listed numerous mistakes he had made.

First, he had brought the subject to the church before he really knew what the Bible taught. He had just seen it in the Bible, heard some other Baptists in various places going to it, so he jumped on the bandwagon really unprepared to do what he tried to do---introduce it and install it in the church.

Second, this had made the presentation of it premature and dangerous for several reasons. For one thing, the idea of elder rule, which came across to his men elected to serve as elders, was that they were all equal in authority and leadership importance. They developed the idea that they were as authoritative as the pastor. Again, his premature presentation of the subject to the church left the church unclear about how an elder ruled church should really operate. All of this led to ignorance as to what they were doing, legalism, and a dangerous pluralism in leadership with no one really leading the church.

Finally, it all came to a head when one elder took the reigns of leadership out of the hands of the pastor, and they fired him. The last straw, he said, was that the elders assured him they were the ones who led the church---not the pastor. He was only another one of the elders, subject to their authority. This certainly agreed with the story told by Todd.

When he had finished, I asked him why he had called me. I reminded him of the trouble he had tried to start in my church by his arrogance, and the lousy attitude he demonstrated when I had given him an opportunity to preach in my church. And I also faced him with the damage he had done in Todd's life, and noted the damage may not be over if he marries a girl out of God's will, and if he gets hurt as the new pastor at Middleville.

With that he hung his head, and then with a tear or two in his eyes, he apologized to me for his actions. He agreed great damage had been done to the church and the men, and that even further damage could be done to Todd, and even Jane. He asked what he could do to change these things which had risen from his ignorance and sin.

I admitted to him that I had no answer to that question. I had learned in the ministry that you do not correct the bitter and sorrowful results of sinful actions in a church or ministry simply by saying, "I was wrong!" That is a beginning, but sometimes the damage is so great, that one can only pray and trust God to work matters out. I did set before him the need to go to all parties involved and confess his sin and ignorance, even Middleville Baptist Church, the elders there, Todd and Jane, my church, and any other place where he had preached his arrogant sermon or pulled his immature trick.

After we prayed, I assured him I would be available to talk with him any time about any matter.

Then he floored me with his next question.

"Brother Ira, do you think it would be acceptable for me to join your church so you could work with me? I need a church for myself and my family and my future. I must prove myself in some place. Could I put myself under your authority, leadership and training so you could work with me and then judge when I am ready to go back into a pastorate?"

I asked myself what all this could entail or lead to? Would he, come in and bring disunity to Unity Baptist Church again? How could I know I could trust him? Did he have his eye on my pulpit? Would it pose a problem that I had people in my church who were related to him? What about the people who were not in favor of elder rule? Would they think his coming to our church was a sure sign we were going to elder rule? Or if I began to seek to lead our church into elder rule (the Biblical kind), would he take it up as a crusade, and seek to push and promote it in a premature manner, or would he leave the matter completely in my hands and keep his mouth shut---and I mean shut!

Then I faced him with these questions! He accepted the matter with understanding, and with some disappointment. He then agreed to look elsewhere for guidance and help.

As he sat before me, though, I ached for him. But I was cautious for our Lord's church. If only I could be sure of his motives and sincerity!

As I drove home, I wondered why all the problem people come to me? Then I was ashamed of that thought. Isn't that what the ministry is---helping sinners, even ministerial failures?

When I got home, I called Billy and told him I would work with him---but only under the strictest of conditions, which I laid down for him. Some of them made marine training look like romper room games. If he choked on them, so be it. But he didn't, and the day ended with my having another family for the church, but hardly the average "bear," or new member or members, I mean!

Now I wondered what Todd would say!

44

Where Do We Go from Here...?

After resting awhile in the afternoon, I felt a need to summarize some of my conclusions concerning what I had seen in my study on church government.

1. The Old Testament people of God were led by elders.

2. The Jews of the New Testament period were led by elders also.

3. The New Testament people of God were also led by elders.

4. The office of deacon was never an office of leadership but one of service.

5. There was a plurality of elders in the New Testament church.

6. There was the office of pastor/teacher in the New Testament church.

7. The pastor/teacher was the one who primarily handled the Word of God in the New Testament church.

8. The pastor/teacher was an elder, but not all elders were pastor/teachers.

9. Some elders carried primarily the responsibility of leadership and not the handling of the Word.

10. The pastor/teacher also was to be the leader of the elders, since he was the one gifted in the handling of the Word of God.

11. There are clear qualifications given in the New Testament for those who would serve as elders.

12. There is a definite attitude of love and humility, etc. required in the service of the elders.

13. There is a definite attitude of love, respect and obedience demanded of the people for their elders.

14. There is not to be given to the elders a blind loyalty or obedience, as if the elders can violate the Word of God in their demands or take the place of the Holy Spirit in the member's life.

14. There is the possibility of a member bringing an accusation against an elder, thus indicating the elders must have a standard of correct conduct and the members a structure of accountability.

I also listed some suggestions which had come to mind concerning the establishment and functioning of elder leadership in a church.

The one or ones leading a church to elder rule must:

1. Take great care in moving a church to elder leadership---it cannot be rushed

2. Be absolutely certain of what an elder-led church is. One cannot lead a church to elder leadership and learn the system as one goes, or find the answers in the process. Every aspect possible must be studied and anticipated.

3. Realize that many churches are presently using their deacons as elders.

4. Understand where the people are in their thinking about this subject and meet them there.

5   Understand there will be much misunderstanding, misrepresentation, and confusion on the subject, and never get upset, over-zealous or impatient in introducing the subject and teaching the people about it.

6.. Take special and careful pains to educate the people in a slow process, seeking to answer all questions, not forcing any thing down their throats.

7. Assure the people what elder rule is and what it is not. Fear and ignorance of the known and the unknown has scuttled many a proper action.

8. Present the material in a smaller group.

9. Do not present it initially and primarily in the morning worship service.

10. Never make the issue a defining issue of one's ministry. If the church accepts elder leadership--- fine. If the church does not---so be it. Many churches have done great things for God without being elder-led.

Following the acceptance of elder leadership, be sure the following is done:

1. Keep the people informed of the work of the elders. May it never be said by the members that they have no idea what the elders are doing or where the church is going. Eldership is not a secret Gnostic society for an elite few. Elders are leaders of the church, answerable to God, yes, but also to the people.

2. Get the people's commitment for the work of the church, especially new programs. Don't expect the people to rubber stamp every program the elders present, if they have not been involved in the presentation, planning and promotion of the matter.

3. Involve the people in church discipline. This is Scriptural. They must know the issues concerning discipline. They are even to be given a voice of approval concerning disciplinary action. Discipline is not the duty of the elders alone.

4. Remember that elders who act alone may be left standing alone because they have demanded a blind loyalty from the people, asking them to rubber stamp their ideas and opinions when the people may not even know the issues or reasons for an issue or action.

I looked back over my list, and then asked the Lord to give me wisdom in presenting the subject in my church. There had to be, I was convinced, clear understanding of the responsibilities of the people to the elders (with accountability of the people to the elders), clear understanding of the responsibilities of the elders to the people (with accountability of the elders to the people), and clear understanding of the responsibilities of the pastor/teacher (with accountability also on his part to the church as well). Failure to understand the responsibilities, and failure to have accountability procedures, would cause the whole system to fail.

Yes, I was now convinced of elder leadership in the New Testament church, but not of everything every body thought the term "elder rule" meant.

Just like every other doctrinal subject, if someone were to ask me if I believed in elder rule, I would ask them, "What do you think elder rule is?" I would refuse to believe any one's false ideas or concepts of any doctrinal subject just because they used a familiar byword or identifying tag.

45

What About Everything Else...?

I did get back into the pulpit the next Sunday, and what a joy it was after several weeks' absence. In several months I was back to full health, stronger than ever, Terry said.

I also presented elder rule in Unity Baptist Church, in the manner and with the convictions I have set forth in this book. When we were finished (it took more than a year to educate the people), it was almost a hundred per cent vote that we adopt elder leadership in our church. Even Mrs. Palmer voted for elder rule.

Troy Medford did work through his sad and moving experience concerning his mother, Mandy Collier. I preached her funeral, and marveled that many times the gospel of Jesus Christ gets the last word as one leaves this world. It was a sad funeral, however. There are no sadder words than "what could have been."

Phil Millow got out of jail quickly after Mandy's suicide. The evidence did not stand up against him. He came back to church, dedicated his life anew, and is growing in the Lord now. Though I would not suggest that pathway, it is true many times, that the greater the sins forgiven, the greater the love in response.

The Dink and the boys are still in church, growing in a way that continues to amaze us all. Dink thinks the Lord may be calling him to preach now. I am praying about using him in a jail ministry, if he is serious about his call.

Todd got married, and is still pastoring Middleville Baptist Church. Only time will tell what will become of both of those relationships---the wife and the church.

Billy Motley is still in our church. He did exactly as he promised when I faced him with the standards of conduct demanded, if I was to work with him. I think he may be ready to go back into the ministry soon.

And I must admit, I am enjoying some free time now that this third doctrinal quest has been settled! But not for long, because we got word today that Terry is expecting our first child. Can you imagine that---Ira, Jr., perhaps.

But I guess I can't get too comfortable. I have a feeling that a new doctrinal pursuit will raise its head any day now!

I still want to chase the subject of eschatology, but it seems the Lord chooses these studies for me in light of events He brings into my life. Plus eschatology is so controversial! Maybe I will wait and finalize all my thinking on that subject just before I die---then if people yell at me, I can take it better, for I will know who was right and who was wrong on that area of doctrine.

Whatever, I think I will be back in the saddle of pursuit again soon. I don't think I'll wait as long before I take off again, as I did between the first two and this one!